THE KNITTER'S GUIDE TO

Yarn Cocktails

THE KNITTER'S GUIDE TO

Yarn Cocktails

30 Technique-Expanding Recipes for Tasty Little Projects

GLOUCESTER MASSACHUSETTS

QUARRY BOOKS

Anastasia Blaes and Kelly Wilson

First published in the United States of America by
Quarry Books, a member of
Quayside Publishing Group
33 Commercial Street
Gloucester, Massachusetts 01930-5089
Telephone: (978) 282-9590
Fax: (978) 283-2742
www.quarrybooks.com

Library of Congress Cataloging-in-Publication Data
Blaes, Anastasia.
   The knitter's guide to yarn cocktails : 30 technique-expanding recipes for tasty little projects / Anastasia Blaes and Kelly Wilson.
      p.   cm.
   ISBN-13: 978-1-59253-319-0
   ISBN-10: 1-59253-319-1
   1. Knitting—Patterns. I. Wilson, Kelly. II. Title.
TT825.B5465 2007
746.43'2041—dc22   2006035268
                                                         CIP

ISBN-13: 978-1-59253-319-0
ISBN-10: 1-59253-319-1

10 9 8 7 6 5 4 3 2 1

Design: Judy Morgan
Photography: Allan Penn, except for pages 28, 32, 44, 49, 50, 71, 75, 89, 109, 113, and 116 by
   Glenn Scott Photography
Illustrations: Judy Love
Technical Editing and Schematics: Sue McCain

Printed in China

Yarns shown on cover (Left to Right): Cascade Venezia in #111, Blue Heron Yarns Rayon Metallic in Hibiscus, Mountain Colors Wooly Feathers in Wild Raspberry, Kolláge Yarns Inspiration in Hot to Trot, South West Trading Company Phoenix in Mermaid Mix

To the Blaes boys—A.B.

To Mom and Dad—K.W.

Menu

Introduction

Welcome to the *Yarn Cocktails* Lounge!

Looking for some cool refreshment? Unwind after a long, hard day with a *Yarn Cocktails* pattern!

Inspired by popular drinks, *Yarn Cocktails* patterns are relaxing designs for knitters that explore new techniques in tasty sips. Each pattern focuses on a specific technique, so you can slow down and fully master a new skill while savoring the sensuous process of using luscious yarns to create a unique, touchable cocktail.

Knitting is uniquely personal. The alchemy of fingers and needles, color and fiber, casts its spell, elevating the practical to the sublime. Many methods will achieve this result: it's up to you to choose which you prefer. We will show you our favorites.

To guide you, the *Yarn Cocktails* menu (see previous page) is divided according to drink category and technique. Experienced knitters can browse the menu to select a project for their knitted refreshment; knitters who wish to expand their skills will find a detailed explanation of each technique at the beginning of each chapter. Projects become more challenging as the chapter goes on, introducing new applications of each technique. In turn, each chapter builds on the skills learned in the previous one. This step-by-step approach will prepare even beginning knitters for intricate projects. By the time you have completed all the projects, you will be an accomplished knitter with a wardrobe full of your own handmade, luxurious creations!

As you read through the chapters, symbols will guide you. Not sure if you've learned the techniques needed to complete the project? Look for the ice cube at the top of the pattern, which will list the techniques needed to successfully complete the project and where they are located in the book. Olives at the top of the pattern indicate its difficulty level: the more olives, the more challenging the project. For designer tips that will give your creation a professional finish, check out the martini glasses.

Yarn Cocktails projects are relaxing, instructive, and portable, perfect for busy lifestyles. They offer something for everyone, from boxer shorts and neckties for the men to necklaces and skirts for the ladies. So, have a seat, kick off your shoes, and quench your thirst for knitted refreshment with *Yarn Cocktails* designs!

& *Kelly*

www.anatasiaknits.com

Ingredients

TOOLS OF THE TRADE

Although knitting needles can be found in a wide variety of materials and styles, all of them have at least one pointed end and a straight length for holding (see illustrations on page 11 of knitting needles with labeled parts). Either the packaging or the needle itself will be labeled with the needle size. For the U.S. sizes, the larger the number, the bigger the diameter of the needle. The actual measurement of the diameter of the needles is labeled in millimeters (mm) on the needles or the package as well, and is generally the most consistent way to determine needle size.

KNITTING NEEDLE SIZES

U.S.	Metric
1	2.25 mm
2	2.75 mm
3	3.25 mm
4	3.5 mm
5	3.75 mm
6	4 mm
7	4.5 mm
8	5 mm
9	5.5 mm
10	6 mm
10½	6.5 mm
11	8 mm
13	9 mm
15	10 mm
17	12.75 mm
19	15 mm
35	19 mm
50	25 mm

Source: www.yarnstandards.com

Needle Materials

Knitting needles can be found in a wide variety of materials and styles. You can even find fancy sticks fashioned from glass and ebony! These differences enable you to choose the needle that's best for your project.

Aluminum—These needles are slippery and can make for noisy knitting when an enthusiastic knitter clicks her needles instead of her heels.

Bamboo—Lightweight and warm to the touch, these needles are great for sensitive hands.

Wooden—Stitches don't slip off as quickly with these needles, which makes them great for beginners.

Plastic—Light-color needles work well with darker yarns. In contrast, translucent needles work well with eyelash and other novelties. Plastic needles are also lightweight.

10

Brass/Nickel—Slick and fast, these needles are better for experienced knitters. Stitches are quick to jump off the needles.

What's Your Style?

Straight—Most commonly the needle is round, but it may also be square. This type of needle is useful for creating flat pieces of fabric. The point is at one end and a stopper is at the opposite end to prevent stitches from slipping off.

Double-Pointed—These have points at each end and come in sets of 4 or 5 needles. Use double-pointed needles for circular or flat knitting. Beginners will enjoy using wooden or bamboo double-pointed needles for socks because the stitches stay on the needles better.

Circular—Two needles with ends attached by a nylon or elastic flexible cord make up a circular needle. The cord transition to the needles should be smooth, for frustration-free knitting. To tame the flexible nylon cord in circular needles, dip it in hot water and reshape.

Tapestry Needles (also called yarn needles)—These are very useful for weaving in ends and sewing seams. They should have a blunt point to avoid splitting the yarn, and an eye large enough for the yarn that will be threaded through them.

STRAIGHT
stopper
needle
point

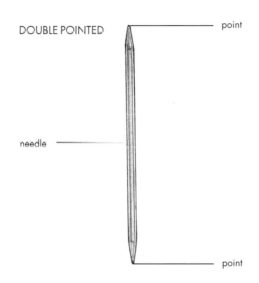

DOUBLE POINTED
point
needle
point

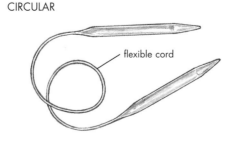

CIRCULAR
flexible cord

Tips

- You can make your metal knitting needles smoother and faster by rubbing hand lotion or waxed paper over them.

- Keep knitting needles stored away from small children and damp, dark locations. The original packaging or a needle case is an ideal storage place for them when not in use.

Embroidery Needles—These are smaller needles that are good for weaving in ends of smaller yarns and threads; used when the large eye of a tapestry needle would leave holes in the fabric.

Cable Needles—Use these small needles to hold stitches at the front or back of your knitting while you work other stitches and then come back to the ones on the cable needles. Cable needles come in several different styles and materials, from a bamboo double-pointed needle to a metal hook.

Crochet Hooks—Even if you don't know how to crochet, these handy hooks will be of use to you. They make applying fringe a breeze and are wonderful for picking up dropped stitches.

11

Stitch and Row Markers—These can be closed or split rings made specifically for knitting or crochet, or you may substitute a length of contrasting color yarn, tied into a small ring. Place a marker where there's a change in stitch pattern or to catch your attention when you need to do something different, such as an increase or decrease. Split ring markers are open rings that slide onto stitches and can be removed easily. Use them to indicate the front side of your knitting or place them at ten-row intervals to make counting rows easier. Coilless safety pins or a length of yarn will also do the trick.

Point Protectors—We like the rubber ones. Place these onto the points of your needles to prevent stitches from slipping off. As you might imagine, point protectors are particularly useful for double-pointed needles. A rubber band wrapped around the tip of the needle works great if a point protector isn't handy.

Stitch Holder—This looks like a large safety pin. If you prefer, use a length of contrasting color yarn to hold live stitches safely until they are needed again.

Row Counter or Paper and Pencil—Keep track of how many rows you've completed with these basic tools.

Sticky Notes or Magnetic Board with Magnet—Use these to keep your place in a pattern or chart.

Ruler—Measure the stitches and rows of your knitting with a ruler or, if you prefer, a dressmaker's tape measure. A gauge tool has a right angle cutout that makes this easy.

Hand Lotion—A good cream will keep your hands and cuticles soft. Some hand lotions will stain and feel greasy. Look for a product that is made with hand knitters in mind (see Resources on page 157).

Coilless Safety Pins—Unlike regular safety pins, these are missing the extra loop of wire at the bend, which can trap fibers and snag yarns.

Rustless Pins—Block your knitting with these pins, which will hold your knitted fabric in place while it's drying on the blocking board.

Blocking Board—Lay out your damp knitted piece on this board for blocking and drying. It's very helpful if it has a grid or squares to keep things straight. If you like, you can also use the top of a bed.

Spray Bottle—Dampen the knitted piece with a spray bottle, then wrap it in a towel to remove the excess water before blocking. A steam iron may also be used to block your piece. Lay the piece wrong side up. Do not press the iron down on the fabric, but instead, hold it above the fabric, using the steam setting, and keep it moving.

Scissors—Always keep them sharp and in a safe place.

Yarn Swift—This clever contraption holds a hank of yarn and expands to fit different-size hanks. It spins around as yarn is pulled off to be wound into a center-pull ball. It is often used in conjunction with a ball winder, which quickly winds the yarn off the swift.

Center-Pull Ball—Thread the yarn through the guide of a ball winder and secure. Turn the crank and create a ball that pulls from the inside. This ball won't roll around. Handspinners will know of a tool called the *nostepinne.* It does the

Tips

- When winding a center-pull ball, take care to let the yarn wind on loosely. Do not pull the yarn tightly while turning the crank. When you pull the ball off of the winder, the center should not collapse. If it does, it's wound too tightly. Tight balls put stress on the yarn, which causes it to lose resilience. You may wash the yarn, but if you do, do it before knitting with it or the garment may shrink when the yarn goes back to having its original bounce.

- If you enjoy the knitted jewelry projects in this book, you may want to invest in tools like chain-nose pliers and round-nose pliers.

same job but takes longer, since you're winding the ball by hand. You may also wind a ball around your hand. Wrap a long tail around your thumb, then wrap the yarn around your fingers. The long tail will pull from the center when the ball is complete.

Beads—Beads come in an endless variety of shapes, sizes and materials. Round and smooth beads, such as pearls, are the most common type. Some beads have facets, areas that are smooth and flat, just like on a diamond, which reflect light for a glitzy look. Bicone beads have two points, one at each end of the bead. Teardrops look just like a tear, and may be smooth or faceted. Chips are small irregular-shaped beads. Regardless of the shape of the bead, its size is determined by measuring its diameter in millimeters (mm). Our favorite beads are made out of crystal, glass, and natural materials such as stone and wood. Holes that are drilled into beads can be different diameters, too. This is important to remember when pairing beads with yarn or thread. Make sure to choose a stringing material that will comfortably fit through the bead hole.

Stringing Materials—Choose stringing materials that will work well with the diameter of the beads you are using and are strong enough for the weight of the beads. Examples are clear nylon cord or transite, beading wire, silk cord, and nylon or silk thread.

Jeweler's Glue—This is a contact cement with a fine-tip applicator at the end of the tube. It is easy to find in bead shops and is very useful for securing knots. Just apply a drop of the glue to the cut end of your beading thread or cord and allow it to dry. Clear nail polish may also be used, but we've found it to gum up and discolor some yarns. We've also tried some of the quick-dry gel glues, but they damaged the finish of some beads. You want your pieces to be secure and look great. Jeweler's glue is your best bet.

Flexible Twisted Wire Beading Needle—The eye of this beading needle collapses when beads pass over it. The wire bends and is very flexible.

#10 Rigid Beading Needle—This type of needle does not bend. It is good for stringing small beads with thread.

Jewelry Findings—A few of the components that give a jewelry piece its structure are earring wires, clasps, and knot covers.

Earring Wires—These are, of course, used to make earrings. Popular styles are the fish hook and leverback hinged.

Clasps—The ends of a necklace or bracelet are connected together with these. Popular styles of clasps are the toggle, box, and magnetic.

Knot Covers (also called bead tips)—Use these at the end of a jewelry piece to hide a knot.

SHAKEN OR STIRRED? MIXING A *YARN COCKTAILS* DESIGN PROPERLY

Once you have your tools, you are ready to get some "mixers," those scrumptious yarns you will use to make your *Yarn Cocktails* design. For best results, use the yarns listed under the "Shown" heading of each project. If you choose to substitute a different yarn, select one that has similar gauge and fiber properties, or you may be in for an unpleasant surprise. For example, if you select cotton for a project that specifies wool, your beautiful skirt will sag and droop like a wilted flower rather than flatter your figure. Why? Because cotton is not an elastic fiber; it doesn't bounce back to hold its shape. Wool's crimp makes it naturally elastic, thus wool is a better choice for a skirt, which needs to be flexible. It's also important to consider yarn texture. If you are working on a *Yarn Cocktails* design with a basketweave pattern and you substitute a furry yarn for a smooth-textured yarn, the fur will obscure the stitch detail—and all of your hard work.

YARN SUBSTITUTIONS GUIDE—STANDARD YARN WEIGHT SYSTEM

Categories of yarn, gauge ranges, and recommended needle and hook sizes

Yarn weight symbols and category names	**1** Super Fine	**2** Fine	**3** Light	**4** Medium	**5** Bulky	**6** Super Bulky
Types of yarns in category	sock, fingering, baby	sport, baby	DK, light worsted	worsted, afghan, aran	chunky, craft, rug	bulky, roving
Knit gauge range° in stockinette stitch to 4" (10 cm)	27–32 sts	23–26 sts	21–24 sts	16–20 sts	12–15 sts	6–11 sts
Recommended needle in metric size range	2.25–3.25 mm	3.25–3.75 mm	3.75–4.5 mm	4.5–5.5 mm	5.5–8 mm	8 mm and larger
Recommended needle in U.S. size range	1 to 3	3 to 5	5 to 7	7 to 9	9 to 11	11 and larger
Crochet gauge° ranges in single crochet to 4" (10 cm)	21–32 sts	16–20 sts	12–17 sts	11–14 sts	8–11 sts	5–9 sts
Recommended hook in metric size range	2.25–3.5 mm	3.5–4.5 mm	4.5–5.5 mm	5.5–6.5 mm	6.5–9 mm	9 mm and larger
Recommended hook U.S. size range	B/1 to E/4	E/4 to 7	7 to I/9	I/9 to K/10½	K/10½ to M/13	M/13 and larger

Source: www.yarnstandards.com

°GUIDELINES ONLY: The above reflects the most commonly used gauges and needle or hook sizes for specific yarn categories.

Fibers

Need more fiber in your diet? Here are some examples of the many fibers you can choose from. Each fiber has its own unique properties that make it both a challenge and a pleasure to work with. Photos show how the yarn looks by itself and how it looks when knitted.

Alpaca

Shown: Blue Sky Alpacas Alpaca and Silk in #136 Champagne and #133 Blush

Properties
- Soft and silky
- Durable and strong
- Lustrous
- Warm—seven times warmer than wool!
- Lighter than wool and drapes beautifully
- Nonallergenic—people who can't wear wool can usually wear alpaca

Challenges
- Slippery on needles
- Not as crimpy as wool and therefore more inelastic

Angora

Shown: Tahki Stacy Charles Jolie Angora in #5004

Properties
- Warm
- Lightweight
- Soft
- Drapes beautifully
- Hydroscopic—wicks moisture away from the body

Challenges
- Inelastic
- May felt if subjected to friction
- Slippery on needles
- A tight knitter will crush the fiber and won't get a nice halo

Cashmere

Shown: Tahki Stacy Charles Filatura Di Crosa Scozia Cashmere in #302245

Properties
- Silky soft
- Elastic
- Similar properties to wool

Challenges
- Prone to pilling
- Not durable

Cotton

Shown: Blue Sky Alpacas Dyed Cotton in Honeydew #602

Properties
- Can be reshaped when wet
- Soft
- Absorbent
- Nonallergenic

Challenges
- Heavy when wet and stretches out of shape
- Prone to pilling

Mohair

Shown: Plymouth Yarn Company Le Fibre Nobili Imperiale Super Kid Mohair in #4102

Properties
- Lustrous
- Durable
- Similar to wool

Challenges
- Does not felt as well as wool

17

Rayon

Shown: Blue Heron Yarns Rayon Softwist in Kelp

Properties
- Processed from wood pulp and acts like a natural fiber
- Is very similar to cotton but more absorbent
- Lightweight
- Has breathability
- Drapes well

Challenges
- Will stretch out of shape
- Inelastic
- When wet, it loses great a deal of strength

Silk

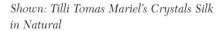

Shown: Tilli Tomas Mariel's Crystals Silk in Natural

Properties
- Cultivated silk is lustrous
- Wild silk can be a golden matte
- Very strong
- Drapes beautifully
- Hydroscopic—wicks moisture away from the body, which makes it good for garments that span the seasons

Challenges
- Inelastic
- Unforgiving—shows differences in tension easily
- Will pill

Wool

Shown: Cascade Yarns Cascade 220 Wool in #9421

Properties
- Warm
- Elastic
- Wicks moisture

Challenges
- Some people are allergic to wool
- Depending on the quality, wool may feel very soft or quite harsh and scratchy

Alternative Fibers

Here are some fibers that add interest to your diet.

Corn

Soy

Bamboo

Shown: South West Trading Company aMAIZing in Purple Gum Drop #156

Shown: South West Trading Company Oasis Soy in #502 Harvest

Shown: South West Trading Company Bamboo in Sahara #142

Properties
- Environmentally friendly
- Durable
- Lustrous
- Naturally antibacterial

Challenges
- Yarn may split while knitting

Properties
- Environmentally friendly
- Easy care, machine washable and dryable
- Durable
- Resilient
- Silky soft
- Drapes beautifully
- Dye won't bleed or fade

Challenges
- Not all colors are available due to dye techniques

Properties
- Environmentally friendly
- Soft
- Lustrous
- Drapes beautifully
- Durable

Challenges
- Inelastic
- Fuzzes with friction

DON'T FREE-POUR; DO A GAUGE SWATCH!

Gauge swatches are small pieces you knit first to ensure that your finished garment will be the correct size. You won't know if you're using the right tools and mixers without knitting one, and you could end up with a beautiful pair of ruffled panties that will fit a sumo wrestler perfectly instead of you. A gauge swatch also determines whether the yarn you choose will produce the gauge that is given for 4" (10 cm); make sure your swatch is larger than 4" (10 cm) square to get a good measurement. The larger the swatch, the more accurate the gauge.

The knitting needle sizes specified in each pattern's Ingredients list are a starting point. As you knit more, you may notice that your stitches are consistently tighter or looser than the gauge requires. Try swatching with larger needles if you have more stitches per inch (or cm) than the gauge requires. On the other hand, if you don't have enough stitches per inch (or cm) in your swatch, smaller needles might do the trick.

Once you've knitted your gauge swatch, measure it accurately. Make sure you include half and quarter stitches as you measure. One half stitch per 4" (10 cm) may not seem like much, but if you multiply that by, say, 9 when knitting a piece to fit a 36" (91.5 cm) bust, your garment will end up 4½" (11.5 cm) too big! And just because you have the correct gauge at the beginning of a project, don't assume that it will stay that way throughout the project. Continue to check your gauge as you are knitting. Stressful days at work may cause you to pull more on the yarn, resulting in tighter stitches, or you may work a little looser on the weekends. We can't say it enough, check gauge and check gauge. Don't make a *Yarn Cocktails* pattern you can't enjoy!

SKILL LEVELS

Beginner	Projects for first-time knitters using basic knit and purl stitches. Minimal shaping.
Easy	Projects using basic stitches, repetitive stitch patterns, simple color changes, and simple shaping and finishing.
Intermediate	Projects with a variety of stitches, such as basic cables, lace, simple intarsia, double-pointed needles, knitting-in-the-round needle techniques, mid-level shaping and finishing.
Experienced	Projects using advanced techniques and stitches, such as short rows, Fair Isle, more intricate intarsia, cables, lace patterns, and numerous color changes.

Source: www.yarnstandards.com

ABBREVIATIONS

beg—beginning

BO—bind off

C2BW—slip next st to cn and hold in back, p1, p1 from cn

C2FW—slip next st to cn and hold in front, p1, p1 from cn

C4B—slip 2 sts to cn and hold in back, k2, k2 from cn

C4F—slip 2 sts to cn and hold in front, k2, k2 from cn

circ—circular

cm—centimeter(s)

cn—cable needle

CO—cast on

cont—continue

dcd—double centered decrease: slip 2 sts as if to knit 2 sts together, k1, pass 2 slipped sts over

dec—decrease

dpn(s)—double-pointed needle(s)

est—established

g—gram(s)

inc(s)—increase(s)

inc 1—increase 1 st

inc 1-L—left-slanting increase

inc 1-R—right-slanting increase

inc 1-P—increase 1 st in purl

k—knit

k2tog—knit 2 sts together

k3tog—knit 3 sts together

kf&b—knit in the front and back of a stitch

m—meter(s)

mb—make bobble

MC—main color

mm—millimeter(s)

oz—ounce(s)

p—purl

p2tog—purl 2 sts together

p2tog-tbl—purl 2 sts together through back loops

pm—place marker

psso—pass slipped st over

rem—remain (s) (ing)

rep—repeat

rev—reverse

rnd(s)—round(s)

RS—right side

sk2p—slip 1 st, knit 2 sts together, pass slipped st over

sl—slip

sm—slip marker

sp2p—slip 1 st, purl 2 sts together, pass slipped st over

ssk—slip 2 sts, one at a time, knit the 2 slipped sts together

st(s)—stitch(es)

St st Stockinette stitch

T2B—slip next st to cn and hold in back, k1, p1 from cn

T2F—slip next st to cn and hold in front, p1, k1 from cn

tcd—triple centered decrease: slip 2 sts as if to knit 2 sts together, knit next 2 sts together, pass 2 slipped sts over

WS—wrong side

wyib—with yarn in back

wyif—with yarn in front

yd(s)—yard(s)

yo—yarn over

Classic Cocktails

Make Your Own Textural Melody

Textured knitting has a musical quality to it, a rhythm that transfers itself from paper to your fingers. Knit, knit, purl, purl, knit, purl, knit—just saying the words has a percussive feel to it. The interplay of knit and purl stitches energizes a garment, as you will soon find out for yourself.

Texture not only adds excitement to your knitting, it also shapes and stabilizes the garment. Ribbing is a classic example. Vertical stripes of texture, ribbing adds a three-dimensional quality to your knitting. Alternate from a knit stitch to a purl stitch for 1 × 1 ribbing. When going from a knit stitch to the purl stitch, be sure to move your working yarn to the front between the points of the knitting needles. Return your working yarn to the back before working the next knit stitch. If you alternate two knit stitches and two purl stitches, this results in another classic, the 2 × 2 ribbing.

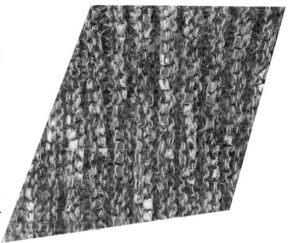

Ribbing adds elasticity, and it forms an excellent border that won't roll. It's great for necklines, the bottoms of sweaters, and the edges of sleeves. Used all over, it makes a form-fitting garment.

Shake things up a little with basketweave. Just take the classic ribbing a step further. Work a group of several knit stitches, then a group of several purl stitches. Once you've worked enough rows to form blocks of all knit and all purl (purl the wrong side of knit stitches, and knit the wrong side of purls), change the order of the groups for a checkerboard pattern that adds an upbeat tempo to your project.

When basic knit and purl stitches are worked simultaneously to form a counterpoint within a garment, the possibilities are endless. The only thing that will be flat about your finished project will be the edges!

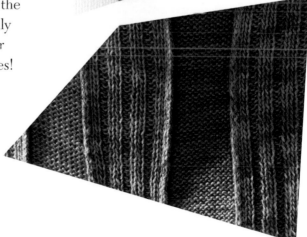

Singapore Sling Bandeau

*Turn heads in this hot bandeau, which hugs your curves with vertical ribbing.
Work it from side to side, then add ties to secure at the back of the neck.
A gorgeous multistrand yarn adds the perfect combination of glam and glitz.
Hot to trot!*

Finished Size

XSmall (Small, Medium, Large)
24 (28, 32, 36)" [61 (71, 81.5, 91.5)
cm] wide × 7½ (8½, 8½, 9)" [19
(21.5, 21.5, 23) cm] high
To fit 28 (32, 36, 40)" [71 (81.5, 91.5,
101.5) cm] bust
Size shown: Medium

Ingredients

231 (294, 336, 441) yds [211 (269,
307, 403) m] medium-weight
mohair/viscose yarn ❹

One pair size 7 (4.5 mm) straight
knitting needles, or size to obtain
gauge

Split ring stitch marker

Tapestry needle

Shown: Kolláge Yarns Inspiration
(mohair/viscose/polyamide; 100 yds
[91.5 m] per 60 g hank): Hot to Trot,
3 (3, 4, 5) hanks

Gauge

20 sts and 28 rows = 4" (10 cm) in
Purl Ridge Pattern
Don't free-pour; do a gauge swatch!

Stitch Explanation

Purl Ridge Pattern (use for any
number of sts):
Row 1 (RS): Sl 1, knit to end of
row.
Row 2: Sl 1, knit to end of row.
Rows 3 and 4: Sl 1, purl to end
of row.
Rep Rows 1–4 for pattern.

Note

Slipping the first stitch of each row
will give you a smooth edge.

Bandeau

CO 38 (42, 42, 45) sts. Beg Purl
Ridge Pattern. Work even until
piece measures 24 (28, 32, 36)" [61
(71, 81.5, 91.5) cm] from CO edge,
ending with row 4.
BO all sts, leaving 40" (101.5 cm) tail.

Ties and Edging

Fold piece in half lengthwise, with
CO edge on top of BO edge. Place
marker at fold line. This will mark
the top front center.

Beg at CO edge, pick up and
knit 1 st in each slipped stitch
along top edge (see page 154), ending at marker; with Cable CO (see
page 149), CO 100 sts. BO all sts
knitwise.

For second tie, CO 100 sts, pick
up and knit 1 st in each slipped st
along top edge, beg at center marker
and ending at BO edge. BO all sts
knitwise.

Finishing

Using tail from BO edge, sew CO
and BO edges together to form back
seam. Weave in all ends to WS and
secure.

25

Deep Blue Sea Belt/Scarf

Set sail on a knitting adventure with this basketweave belt or scarf. The belt can be worn inside or outside the belt loops, and combines two different soy yarns in one ocean-worthy colorway. Knits ahoy!

Finished Size

Scarf: 1½" (4 cm) wide × 60" (152.5 cm) long
Belt: 1½" (4 cm) wide × 55½" (141 cm) or desired length

Ingredients

110 yds (100.5 m) medium-weight soy/wool-blend yarn (A) **4**

175 yds (160 m) medium-weight soy yarn (B) **4**

One pair size 7 (4.5 mm) straight knitting needles, or size to obtain gauge

Two 1¼" (3 cm) D-rings (for belt only)

Tapestry needle

Shown: South West Trading Company Karaoke (50% Soysilk, 50% wool; 109 yds [99.5 m] per 50 g ball): #278 Mermaid Mix (A), 1 ball; Phoenix (100% Soysilk; 175 yds [160 m] per 100 g ball): #099 Mermaid Mix (B), 1 ball

Gauge

9 sts and 12 rows = 1½" (4 cm) in Basketweave Pattern
Don't free-pour; do a gauge swatch!

Stitch Explanation

Stripe Sequence: *Work 12 rows in B, then 12 rows in A; rep from * to end of piece.

Basketweave Pattern

(multiple of 9 sts):
Row 1 (WS): K3, p3, k3.
Row 2: P3, k3, p3.
Rows 3 and 4: Rep Rows 1 and 2.
Rows 5 and 7: Rep Row 2.
Row 6: Rep Row 1.
Row 8: Rep Row 1.
Rep Rows 1–8 for pattern.

Scarf

With B, CO 9 sts. Beg Stripe Sequence and Basketweave Pattern. Work even until Stripe Sequence has been worked 21 times, or to desired length. BO all sts. Weave in all ends to WS and secure.

Belt

Work as for scarf, working Stripe Sequence 14 times, or to 1½" (4 cm) from desired length.

Shape Tab

Change to B and St st. Work even for 4 rows.
Dec Row 1: K1, ssk, k3, k2tog, k1—7 sts rem. Purl 1 row.
Dec Row 2: K1, ssk, k1, k2tog, k1—5 sts rem. Purl 1 row.
BO all sts, leaving 12" (30.5 cm) tail.

Belt Finishing

Insert tab through both D-rings. Fold to WS at beg of tab. Using tail, sew tab to WS, being careful not to let sts show on RS.

Tips

- After binding off, you can knot the yarn tails for instant fringe—no need to weave them in!

- Slipping the first st of each row will give you a smooth edge.

Long Island Iced Tea Athletic Socks

Intimidated by socks? Have no fear. Everyone can knit these knee socks . . . on straight needles! We've used ribbing to its fullest potential around the leg and at the heel. You don't even have to know how to turn a heel. Knit up a pair over a weekend and you've got game.

Finished Size

Small (Medium, Large, XLarge)
7¾ (10¼, 11½, 11½)" [19.5 (26, 29, 29) cm] circumference around ball of foot
6½ (8, 9½, 11)" [16.5 (20.5, 24, 28) cm] length from heel to toe
To fit girls' and women's shoe sizes 3/4 (5/6, 7/8, 9/10)
Size shown: Medium (size 5/6 women's shoe)

Ingredients

200 (240, 270, 310) yds [183 (219.5, 247, 283.5) m] super fine–weight wool yarn in blue (MC)

35 (45, 50, 55) yds [32 (41, 45.5, 50.5) m] superfine-weight wool yarn in yellows/greens (A)

One pair size 1 (2.25 mm) straight knitting needles, or size to obtain gauge

Stitch marker

Tapestry needle

Shown: Lorna's Laces Shepherd Sock (80% superwash wool, 20% nylon; 215 yds [196.5 m] per 2 oz [57 g] hank): #51ns Island Blue (MC), 1 (2, 2, 2) hanks; #204 Daffodil (A), 1 hank

Gauge

32 sts and 47 rows = 4" (10 cm) in Stockinette stitch (St st)
Don't free-pour; do a gauge swatch!

Note

Slip all sts purlwise, with yarn in back.

29

Ribbing

With MC, CO 62 (82, 92, 92) sts.

Row 1 (WS): K2, *p3, k2; rep from * to end of row.

Row 2: P2, *k1, sl 1, k1, p2, rep from * to end of row.

Work even until piece measures 1½" (4 cm) from CO edge, ending with Row 2.

Change to A and work even for 2 rows.

Change to MC and work even for ½" (1.3 cm), ending with Row 2.

Change to A and work even for ¾" (2 cm), ending with Row 2.

Change to MC and work even for 8 rows.

Change to A and work even for 2 rows.

Change to MC and work even until piece measures 15" (38 cm) from CO edge or to desired length for calf, ending with Row 1.

Shape Foot

Row 1 (RS): Work 15 (20, 25, 25) sts as established, *p2tog, k1, sl 1, k1*; rep from * to * 5 (7, 7, 7) times, p2tog, work as established to end of row—55 (73, 83, 83) sts rem. Place marker (pm) at beg of row.

Row 2: Work 15 (20, 25, 25) sts, p25 (33, 33, 33), work to end.

Shape Heel

Row 1 (RS): Work 15 (20, 25, 25) sts, k2tog, k21 (29, 29, 29), ssk, work to end of row—53 (71, 81, 81) sts rem.

Row 2: Work 15 (20, 25, 25) sts, p23 (31, 31, 31), work to end of row.

Row 3: Work 15 (20, 25, 25) sts, k2tog, k19 (27, 27, 27), ssk, work to end of row—51 (69, 79, 79) sts rem.

Row 4: Work 15 (20, 25, 25) sts, p21 (29, 29, 29), work to end of row.

Row 5: Work 15 (20, 25, 25) sts, k2tog, k17 (25, 25, 25), ssk, work to end of row—49 (67, 77, 77) sts rem.

Row 6: Work 15 (20, 25, 25) sts, p19 (27, 27, 27), work to end of row.

Row 7: Work 15 (20, 25, 25) sts, k19 (27, 27, 27), work to end of row. Rep Rows 6 and 7 until piece measures 2 (2½, 3, 3 ½)" [5 (6.5, 7.5, 9) cm] from row marker, ending with Row 6.

Foot

Row 1 (RS): Knit.

Row 2: Purl.

Rep Rows 1 and 2 for 3 (3½, 4, 5)" [7.5 (9, 10, 12.5) cm] or until piece measures 1½ (2, 2½, 2½)" [4 (5, 6.5, 6.5) cm] from desired length of foot, ending with Row 2.

Shape Toe

Row 1 (RS): K11 (15, 17, 17), k2tog, ssk, k19 (29, 35, 35), k2tog, ssk, knit to end of row—45 (63, 73, 73) sts rem.

Row 2 and all WS rows: Purl.

Row 3: K10 (14, 16, 16), k2tog, ssk, k17 (27, 33, 33), k2tog, ssk, knit to end of row—41 (59, 69, 69) sts rem.

Row 5: K9 (13, 15, 15), k2tog, ssk, k15 (25, 31, 31), k2tog, ssk, knit to end of row—37 (55, 65, 65) sts rem.

Row 7: K8 (12, 14, 14), k2tog, ssk, k13 (23, 29, 29), k2tog, ssk, knit to end of row—33 (51, 61, 61) sts rem.

Row 9: K7 (11, 13, 13), k2tog, ssk, k11 (21, 27, 27), k2tog, ssk, knit to end of row—29 (47, 57, 57) sts rem.

Row 11: K6 (10, 12, 12), k2tog, ssk, k9 (19, 25, 25), k2tog, ssk, knit to end of row—25 (43, 53, 53) sts rem.

Sizes Medium, Large, and XLarge Only

Row 13: K9 (11, 11), k2tog, ssk, k17 (23, 23), k2tog, ssk, knit to end of row—39 (49, 49) sts rem.

Row 15: K8 (10, 10), k2tog, ssk, k15 (21, 21), k2tog, ssk, knit to end

of row—35 (45, 45) sts rem.

Row 17: K7 (9, 9), k2tog, ssk, k13 (19, 19), k2tog, ssk, knit to end of row—31 (41, 41) sts rem.

Sizes Large and XLarge Only

Row 19: K8, k2tog, ssk, k17, k2tog, ssk, knit to end of row—37 sts rem.

Row 21: K7, k2tog, ssk, k15, k2tog, ssk, knit to end of row—33 sts rem.

Finishing

BO all sts, leaving 36" (91.5 cm) tail. Lightly block pieces, if desired. Fold sides of toe to WS at shaping edges. Using fake grafting method as shown in illustration (below), sew toe seam. Using Mattress St (see page 156), sew bottom of foot seam and continue up ribbing for leg, changing to A to sew the stripes. Weave in all ends to WS and secure.

Make second sock to match first.

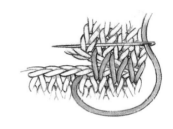

Tips

- When changing colors, cut previous yarn, leaving at least a 6" (15 cm) tail. Join new color by wrapping the new yarn around the right needle to complete the stitch.

- When measuring circumference of foot, wrap tape measure around middle of foot at widest point.

- Make sure to move yarn back and forth between the needle points when working ribbing: to the front before purling, and to the back before knitting.

- When working the Mattress Stitch seam along the bottom of the foot, work into half of the first and last sts of each row, to cut down on seam bulk.

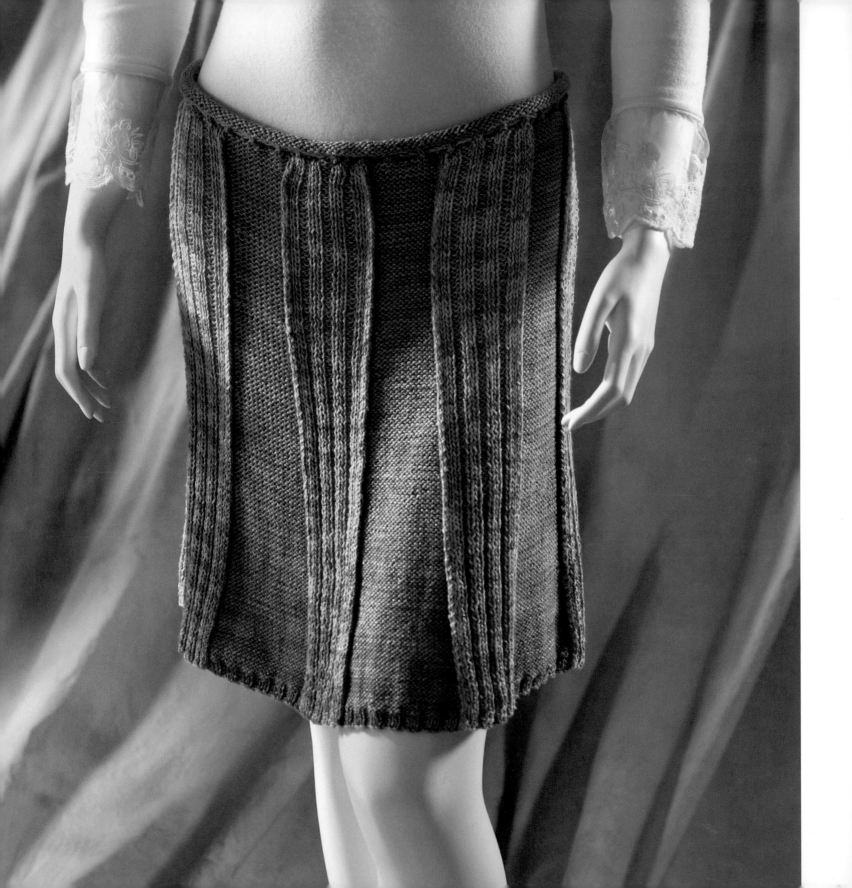

Tequila Sunrise Skirt

Can you make a scarf? Then you can make this fabulous skirt! Alternate ribbed and Stockinette strips, then sew them together to form a tube. A drawstring waistband pulls it all together and adjusts for a perfect fit. The hand-dyed rayon yarn adds a beautiful drape and luscious color. Rise and shine!

Finished Size
Small (Medium, Large, XLarge)
28 (32, 36, 40)" [71 (81.5, 91.5, 101.5) cm] waist circumference, before tightening drawstring
Size shown: Medium

Ingredients
300 (350, 400, 450) yds [274.5 (320, 366, 411.5) m] medium-weight rayon/metallic-blend hand-dyed yarn in yellows/oranges (MC) **4**

434 (487, 554, 607) yds [397 (445.5, 506.5, 555) m] medium-weight rayon/metallic-blend hand-dyed yarn in pinks/purples (A) **4**

2 yds (1.8 m) smooth waste yarn

One pair size 4 (3.5 mm) straight knitting needles, or size to obtain gauge

One size 3 (3.25 mm) 24" (61 cm) -long circular (circ) knitting needle

Row counter

Tapestry needle

Shown: Blue Heron Yarns Rayon Metallic (88% rayon, 12% metallic; 550 yds [503 m] per 8 oz [228 g] hank): Hibiscus (MC), 1 hank; and Sea Star (A), 1 (1, 2, 2) hanks

Gauge
22 sts and 31 rows = 4" (10 cm) in Stockinette stitch (St st) with larger needles
Don't free-pour; do a gauge swatch!

Ribbed Panel
[make 7 (8, 9, 10)]
With larger needles and MC, CO 16 sts.
Row 1 (WS): K1, *p2, k2; rep from * to last 3 sts, p2, k1.
Row 2: P1, *k2, p2; rep from * to last 3 sts, k2, p1.
Work even until piece measures 17 (19, 19, 21)" [43 (48.5, 48.5, 53.5) cm] from CO edge, ending with a WS row. Place sts on length of waste yarn and set aside.
Make total of 7 (8, 9, 10) ribbed panels, using row counter to ensure that each strip is exactly the same length.

33

Reverse Stockinette St Panel [make 7 (8, 9, 10)]

With larger needles and A, CO 32 sts.

Rows 1 and 3 (WS): K3, *p2, k2; rep from * to last 5 sts, p2, k3.

Rows 2 and 4: P3, *k2, p2; rep from * to last 5 sts, k2, p3.

Change to Rev St st, beg with a knit row. Work even for 4 rows.

Dec Row (WS): K2, ssk, knit to last 4 sts, k2tog, k2—30 sts rem. Work even for 8 rows. Rep from * to * 8 times—14 sts rem. Work even until panel has same number of rows as ribbed panel. Place sts on length of waste yarn and set aside.

Make total of 7 (8, 9, 10) Rev St st panels, using row counter to ensure that each strip is exactly the same length.

Finishing

Note: The WS of the ribbed panel begins with k1, p2 and ends with p2, k1; the WS of the Rev St st panel is the St st side. Keep all live sts on waste yarn while working seams. The seams will be visible on the RS of the skirt.

With WS of panels facing, using Mattress St (see page 156), and, working seams 1 st in from each edge, sew panels together, alternating 1 ribbed panel with 1 Rev St st panel, until all panels are sewn together, forming one long piece (see Assembly Diagram). Sew two ends of piece together to form a tube. Turn tube inside out so that RS is facing out.

Waistband

With RS facing, beg at the top of any seam (this will become center back of waistband), transfer all sts from waste yarn to smaller needle—210 (240, 270, 300) sts total. With A, working back and forth on needle, beg on WS row.

Dec Row 1 (WS): *P3, p2tog; rep from * to end of row—168 (192, 216, 240) sts rem.

Eyelet Row: K2, *yo, k2tog; rep from * to last 2 sts, k2. Work even in St st for 11 rows. BO all sts. WS facing, using Mattress St, sew back waistband seam.

Drawstring

With smaller needle and MC, CO 248 (260, 272, 284) sts or desired number. BO all sts knitwise.

Thread drawstring through eyelet row, beg and end on WS at center front. Tie in a bow on WS. Weave in all ends to WS and secure.

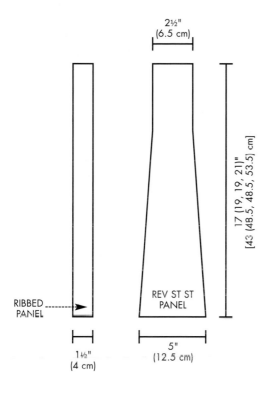

2½"
(6.5 cm)

17 (19, 19, 21)"
[43 (48.5, 48.5, 53.5) cm]

RIBBED
PANEL

REV ST ST
PANEL

1½"
(4 cm)

5"
(12.5 cm)

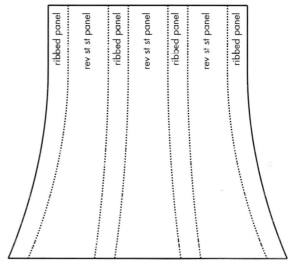

ribbed panel rev st st panel ribbed panel rev st st panel ribbed panel rev st st panel ribbed panel

Note: Dotted lines denote seams. Not all panels are included.
Continue assembling as shown.

Frozen Drinks

Thrills and Chills: A Knitter's Amusement Park

Knitting in the round sounds kind of dangerous, doesn't it? The idea of knitting a seamless tube is thrilling, a roller-coaster ride of spiral stitches where the right side of the project always faces you, you don't have to purl unless you want to, and seaming becomes a distant memory. You choose the thrill level of your knitting amusement park!

Knit every round on one circular needle for a Stockinette stitch ride on the merry-go-round. Take the wheel of a bumper car by purling every round, and you get Reverse Stockinette stitch. Alternate knit and purl rounds if you dare, for a Garter stitch trip into a knitter's fun house. For the adventurous, ride a wild roller coaster as you combine knit and purl stitches within each round.

You can work in the round with a set of four or five double-pointed needles, or with circular needles. If using one circular needle, cast your stitches on normally. Enough stitches need to be on the needle so that they are not stretched to make the connection. If you have to stretch the stitches to make them meet, use double-pointed needles, a shorter circular needle, or two circulars as described below.

Make sure the stitches are arranged so that they aren't twisted when they are joined to form a circle. The illustration below shows a circular needle that has twisted stitches. A twist of lime tastes good

in a Margarita, but twisted cast-on stitches spell trouble in circular knitting. Holding the needles so that the one with the last cast-on stitch is on the right, slip the first cast-on stitch to the right needle and slip the last cast-on stitch to the left-hand needle. Crossing these two stitches helps make a seamless connection. Begin by knitting into the first stitch on the left-hand needle. A closed ring stitch marker (see Tools of the

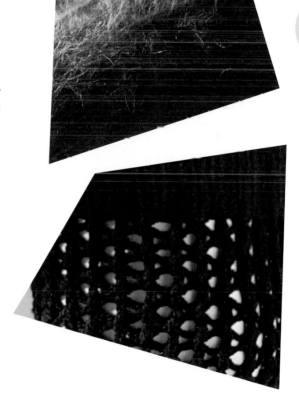

Trade, page 10) placed at the beginning of a round will help keep track of progress.

If you are using double-pointed needles, cast onto a single needle and divide the stitches evenly among the needles. If you are using only four needles, one-third of the stitches should go on the first needle, the second third on the second needle, and the final third on the third needle. Do this counterclockwise, or to the left. The fourth needle remains empty. If using five needles, divide the stitches evenly among four of them, leaving the fifth needle free. As with knitting with one circular needle, make sure that your stitches are not twisted. You should be holding the needle with the last cast-on stitches in your right hand and the needle with the stitches that were first cast on in

your left hand. Bring these two needles to meet, forming a triangle (or square if you are using five needles). Slip the first cast-on stitch to

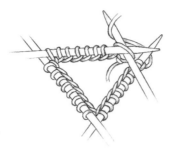

the right-hand needle and slip the last cast-on stitch to the left-hand needle just as you would for joining on circular needles, then insert the empty needle into the first stitch on the left-hand needle to begin. To prevent a line of loose stitches when you move from one needle to another, pull the yarn tighter when going from needle to needle.

For the ultimate thrill ride, try knitting with two circular needles. Cast your stitches onto one circular needle as you normally would. Slip half of these stitches onto the second circular. You will notice that the stitches at the top are now automatically joined. Slide the stitches down the needles from the top to the bottom and turn so that the unjoined stitches are now at the top. Remember, no twisting! Holding the needles so that the one with the last cast-on

stitch is on the right, slip the first cast-on stitch to the right-hand needle and slip the last cast-on stitch to the left-hand needle. Use the bottom tip of the left-hand needle to knit into the first stitch of the left-hand needle.

When all of the stitches on the left-hand needle have been worked, pick up the bottom of the second needle, and knit into the stitches on the second needle. You must always knit your stitches with the bottom tip of the same circular needle.

Whichever method you choose, enjoy the ride!

Watermelon Daiquiri Fingerless Gloves

Fluffy frothy fun is yours as you rib in the round with this luscious angora-blend yarn. Add pizzazz with a novelty yarn at the edges. Details such as an easy thumb gusset and a finger loop complete these delicious gloves.

REFRESH
Textures (page 23)

Finished Size
Circumference: 5½" (14 cm), unstretched; 10" (25.5 cm), stretched

Ingredients
216 yds (197.5 m) lightweight angora/merino-blend yarn (MC) (3)

35 yds (32 m) bulky-weight novelty yarn (A) (5)

1 yd (.9 m) smooth waste yarn

Set of four size 7 (4.5 mm) double-pointed knitting needles (dpn), or size to obtain gauge

Stitch marker

Tapestry needle

Shown: Tahki Yarns Julie (70% French angora, 30% merino wool; 108 yds [99 m] per 25 g ball)· #5023 (MC), 2 balls; Tahki Yarns Poppy (45% nylon, 28% cotton, 27% acrylic; 81 yds [74 m] per 50 g ball): #013 (A), 1 ball

Gauge
29 sts and 30 rows = 4" (10 cm) in 2 × 2 Rib
Don't free pour; do a gauge swatch!

39

THE KNITTER'S GUIDE TO *YARN COCKTAILS*

Stitch Explanation

2 × 2 Rib (multiple of 4 sts):
All Rnds: *P2, k2; rep from * to end of rnd.

Right Glove

With A, CO 40 sts and divide sts onto 3 dpn. Join sts into a circle, being careful not to twist CO edge; place marker (pm) for beg of rnd. *Knit 2 rnds. Purl 2 rnds. Rep from * once.
Change to MC and 2 × 2 Rib. Work even until piece measures 11" (28 cm) from CO edge or to desired length, measuring from base of thumb to 2" (5 cm) above elbow.

Thumb Gusset

Rnd 1: P2, inc 1, k2, inc 1, work to end of rnd—42 sts.
Rnds 2, 4, and 6: Work even, knitting or purling into back of incs.
Rnd 3: P2, k1, inc 1, k2, inc 1, k1, work to end of rnd—44 sts.

Rnd 5: P2, change to waste yarn, k6, transfer last 6 sts worked to left-hand needle, change to MC, k2, *p2, k2; rep from * to end of rnd.
Rnds 6–8: Work even.

Finger Loop

Rnd 9: Work to last 10 sts, CO 14 sts using Backward Loop CO (see page 149), work to end of rnd—58 sts.
Rnd 10: Work to CO sts, BO 14 sts, work to end—44 sts rem.
Rnd 11: Change to A. Knit.
Rnd 12: Purl.
BO all sts loosely knitwise. Weave in all ends to WS and secure.

Thumb

Carefully remove waste yarn and place 12 sts on 3 dpns; pm for beg of rnd. *Note: Beg of rnd should be where first st was worked in waste yarn, on the bottom of the gusset.*
Rnd 1: K6, pick up and knit 1 st from left side of gusset, k6, pick up and knit 1 st from right side of gusset—14 sts. Knit 2 rnds.
Change to A. Knit 1 rnd. Purl 1 rnd. BO all sts loosely knitwise.
Weave in all ends to WS and secure.

Left Glove

Work as for right glove until Rnd 8 of thumb gusset has been completed.

Finger Loop

Rnd 9: Work 10 sts, CO 14 sts using Backward Loop CO, work to end of rnd—58 sts.
Rnd 10: Work to CO sts, BO 14 sts, work to end—44 sts rem.
Complete as for right glove.

Snow Blinder Men's Helmet Hat

This hat protects the neck and ears as well as the top of the head, perfect for playing on the slopes or in the city. Start with an angled Garter Stitch strip, then cast on additional stitches to form a circle. Cover the sensitive neck and ears with a fiber that is both soft and warm.

Finished Size

Small (Medium, Large, XLarge)
Circumference: 17½ (20, 22½, 25)"
[44.5 (51, 57, 63.5) cm]
Size shown: XLarge

Ingredients

200 (200, 225, 250) yds [183 (183, 205.5, 229) m] medium-weight wool yarn (4)

Two size 6 (4 mm) 24" (61 cm) -long circular knitting needles (circ), or size to obtain gauge

(*Optional:* You may use 1 pair size 6 [4 mm] straight needles, 14" [34.5 cm] long, and five size 6 [4 mm] double-pointed needles [dpn], instead of circular needles.)

Stitch marker

Tapestry needle

Shown: Mountain Colors Twizzle (85% merino wool/ 15% silk; 250 yds [225 m] per 100 g hank): Elderberry, 1 hank

Gauge

16 sts and 19 rows = 4" (10 cm) in Stockinette stitch (St st)
Don't free-pour; do a gauge swatch!

Stitch Explanation

Garter Stitch

(any number of sts):
Knit every row.

Garter Stitch in the Round

(any number of sts):
Rnd 1: Purl.
Rnd 2: Knit.
Rep Rnds 1–2 for pattern.

Note

Slip all sts purlwise.

Ear and Neck Flap

With circular or straight needle (optional), CO 32 (34, 38, 42) sts. Working back and forth, beg Garter St as follows:
Row 1: Sl 1 (selvedge st), knit to end of row.
Row 2: Sl 1 (selvedge st), k1, inc 1-R, knit to last st, inc 1-L, k1—34 (36, 40, 44) sts.
Rep Row 2 every row 8 (9, 10, 11) times—50 (54, 60, 66) sts.
Rep Row 1 until piece measures 3" (7.5 cm) or desired length from CO edge.

Cap

(RS) K50 (54, 60, 66). (WS) With Cable CO method (see page 149), CO 20 (26, 30, 34) sts—70 (80, 90, 100) sts. Divide sts between two circular needles or four dpn (optional).

Join sts into a circle, being careful not to twist CO edge; place marker (pm) for beg of rnd. Beg Garter St in the Round. Work even for 5 rnds.

Shape Crown

Dec Rnd 1: *K8, k2tog; rep from * to end of rnd—63 (72, 81, 90) sts rem. Knit 5 (5, 6, 6) rnds.

Dec Rnd 2: *K7, k2tog; rep from * to end of rnd—56 (64, 72, 80) sts rem. Knit 5 (5, 6, 6) rnds.

Dec Rnd 3: *K6, k2tog; rep from * to end of rnd—49 (56, 63, 70) sts rem. Knit 5 (5, 5, 5) rnds.

Dec Rnd 4: *K5, k2tog; rep from * to end of rnd—42 (48, 54, 60) sts rem. Knit 5 (5, 5, 5) rnds.

Dec Rnd 5: *K4, k2tog; rep from * to end of rnd—35 (40, 45, 50) sts rem. Knit 4 (4, 5, 5) rnds.

Dec Rnd 6: *K3, k2tog; rep from * to end of rnd—28 (32, 36, 40) sts rem. Knit 4 (4, 5, 5) rnds.

Dec Rnd 7: *K2, k2tog; rep from * to end of rnd—21 (24, 27, 30) sts rem.

Dec Rnd 8: *K1, k2tog; rep from * to end of rnd—14 (16, 18, 20) sts rem.

Dec Rnd 9: *K2tog; rep from * to end of rnd—7 (8, 9, 10) sts rem.

Finishing

Cut yarn, leaving a 6" (15 cm) tail. Thread tapestry needle with tail and insert through rem sts. Pull to tighten. Weave in ends to WS and secure.

Banana Boat Men's Boxers

Ribbed for your pleasure. Make these boxers for that special someone with a merino yarn that includes polyester and stretchy nylon for elasticity. Worked in a classic rib pattern, with a little short-row shaping to sculpt the rear, the boxers will stretch to conform perfectly to his shape. A hidden drawstring waist ensures a secure fit.

REFRESH
Textures (page 23)

Finished Size

Small (Medium, Large)
Fits waist sizes 32–34 (36–38, 40–42)" [81.5–86.5 (91.5–96.5, 101.5–106.5) cm]
18¾ (21, 23¼)" [47.5 (53.5, 59) cm] waist circumference, unstretched; 32–34 (36–38, 40–42)" [81.5–86.5 (91.5–96.5, 101.5–106.5) cm], stretched
Size shown: Medium
Note: Due to elastic in yarn, boxers will conform to body. Pick size according to waist measurement.

Ingredients

410 (475, 680) yds [375 (434.5, 622) m] medium-weight wool/polyester/nylon-blend yarn in olive green (4)

Two size 8 (5 mm) 16" (40.5 cm) -long circular (circ) knitting needles, or size to obtain gauge

One size 8 (5 mm) 29" (73.5 cm) -long circular (circ) knitting needle

2 stitch markers

Tapestry needle

Shown: GGH Yarns Solitaire (44% merino wool, 43% polyester, 13% elite; 143 yds [130 m] per 50 g ball): #09, 3 (4, 5) balls

Gauge

29 sts and 28 rows = 4" (10 cm) in 2 × 2 Rib
Don't free-pour, do a gauge swatch!

Stitch Explanation

2 × 2 Rib (multiple of 4 sts):
All Rnds: *K2, p2; rep from * to end of rnd.

Note

To add height to the center back of the boxers, we use short-row shaping (see page 151); this will provide adequate coverage of the rear end without increasing the length of the front, and will be seamless.

45

Legs (make 2)

With 16" (40.5 cm) circ needle, CO 88 (96, 104) sts. Join sts into a circle, being careful not to twist CO edge; place marker (pm) for beg of rnd. Beg 2 × 2 Rib; work even until piece measures 5 (5½, 6)" [12.5 (14, 15) cm] from CO edge. Knit first st of next rnd. Transfer last 12 sts worked to waste yarn for crotch. Set aside, leaving rem 76 (84, 92) sts on needle for torso.

Torso

Join Legs

Holding both legs together with sts on waste yarn next to each other, transfer 76 (84, 92) sts from right leg to 29" (73.5 cm) circ needle, pm for center back, transfer 76 (84, 92) sts from left leg to same needle—152 (168, 184) sts (see Assembly Diagram). Join sts into a circle; pm for beg of rnd. Continue in 2 × 2 Rib as established; work even until piece measures 2 (2½, 3)" [5 (6.5, 7.5) cm] from beg of torso.

Shape Torso

Rnd 1: Ssk, work to 2 sts before next marker, k2tog, sl marker (sm), ssk, work to last 2 sts, k2tog—148 (164, 180) sts rem.

Rnds 2 and 3: Work even. Rep Rnds 1–3 three times—136 (152, 168) sts rem. Work even until piece measures 7½ (8, 8½)" [19 (20.5, 21.5) cm] from beg of torso.

Shape Waist

Transfer last 18 (19, 20) sts worked to 16" (40.5 cm) circ needle, then work next 18 (19, 20) sts onto same needle—36 (38, 40) sts. Set aside. These sts will remain inactive while you are working short-row shaping (see page 151) on rem 100 (114, 128) sts.

Row 1: Work to last st, wrap st; turn work. You have placed one st on hold on left side of waist.

Row 2: Rep Row 1. You have placed one st on hold on right side of waist.

Rep Rows 1 and 2 seven (nine, eleven) times—16 (20, 24) sts total placed on hold, 8 (10, 12) sts on either side of waist.

Waistband

Change to working in the round, reactivating all inactive sts. Work in 2 × 2 Rib across all sts, working wraps together with wrapped sts. Work even for 6 rnds. Purl 1 rnd (turning rnd).

Continuing in 2 × 2 Rib, work even for 5 rnds. BO all sts in pattern.

Drawstring

Using 29" (73.5 cm) circ needle, CO 224 sts. BO all sts. *Note: You may adjust length of drawstring if desired by casting on more or less sts.*

Finishing

Folding at turning rnd, fold waistband to WS over drawstring, to form casing. Sew waistband to WS, being careful not to catch drawstring or to let sts show on RS. Turn boxers inside out. Transfer 12 sts on one side of crotch from waste yarn to 16" (40.5 cm) circ needle. Rep for other side on second needle. With 3-Needle BO (see page 156), BO all sts. Weave in all ends to WS and secure.

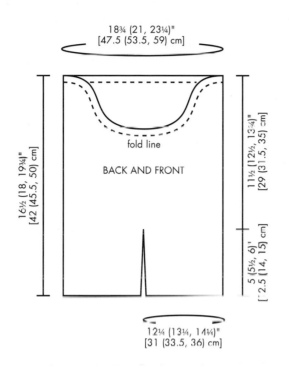

18¾ (21, 23¼)"
[47.5 (53.5, 59) cm]

fold line

BACK AND FRONT

16½ (18, 19¾)"
[42 (45.5, 50) cm]

11½ (12½, 13¾)"
[29 (31.5, 35) cm]

5 (5½, 6)"
[12.5 (14, 15) cm]

12¼ (13¼, 14¼)"
[31 (33.5, 36) cm]

ASSEMBLY DIAGRAM

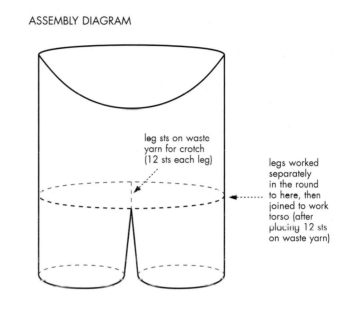

leg sts on waste
yarn for crotch
(12 sts each leg)

legs worked
separately
in the round
to here, then
joined to work
torso (after
placing 12 sts
on waste yarn)

Blackberry Smoothie Stockings

Bring out your inner pinup girl when you flash your gams in these sexy fishnet stockings. The same short-row technique that you used to sculpt the rear of the boxers creates a cup for the heel of the stocking, while an elastic-blend yarn ensures that your stockings will stay up while you dance the night away.

Finished Size

24" (61 cm) long from top of thigh to toe

18–24" (45.5–61 cm) thigh circumference, stretched

Note: Due to elastic in yarn, stockings will stretch to conform to legs.

Ingredients

300 yds (274.5 m) lightweight 98.3% cotton/1.7% elastic-blend yarn in black (**3**)

Set of four size 6 (4 mm) double-pointed knitting needles (dpn), or size to obtain gauge

Stitch marker

Row counter (optional)

Tapestry needle

Shown: Cascade Yarns Fixation (98.3% cotton, 1.7% elastic; 100 yds [91.5 m] per 50 g ball): #8990, 3 balls

Gauge

20 sts and 40 rows = 4" (10 cm) in Stockinette stitch (St st)

Don't free-pour; do a gauge swatch!

Tips

- Get an additional ball of yarn, just in case you run out. This pattern uses every bit of the recommended yardage.

- Use a row counter with this complicated pattern or make tick marks on a piece of paper, so that you don't get lost. Keep track of how many rows you work for each section of the leg, and write it down. When you make your second stocking, you will be able to match it more easily to the first.

- This yarn is very elastic. Don't hold it too taut when knitting your stitches.

Stitch Explanation

2 × 2 Rib (multiple of 4 sts):
All Rnds: *K2, p2; rep from * to end of rnd.

Dcd (double centered decrease): Slip 2 sts together knitwise as if to k2tog, k1, pass 2 slipped sts over—2 sts decreased.

Cuff

CO 64 sts. Divide sts onto 3 needles. Join work into a circle, being careful not to twist sts. Place marker (pm) at beg of rnd.
Beg 2 × 2 Rib. Work even for 20 rnds.

Thigh

Rnd 1: *Yo, dcd, yo, k1; rep from * to end of rnd.
Rnd 2: Knit.
Rnd 3: K1, *yo, k1, yo, dcd; rep from * to last 3 sts, yo, k1, yo, dcd (last 2 sts of this rnd and first st of next rnd); reposition marker after dcd.
Rnd 4: Knit.
Rep Rnds 1–4 five times.

Shape Knee

Rnd 1 (Dec Rnd): Dcd, k1, *yo, dcd, yo, k1; rep from * to end of rnd—62 sts rem.

Rnd 16: Knit.
Rep Rnds 13–16 until piece measures 14½" (37 cm) from CO edge, ending with Rnd 16.

Shape Calf

Rnd 1 (Dec Rnd): Dcd, k1, *yo, dcd, yo, k1; rep from * to end of rnd—54 sts rem.
Rnds 2, 4, 6, 8, 10, 12, 14, 16, 18, and 20: Knit to last st. Do not knit last st.
Rnd 3 (Dec Rnd): Dcd (last st of previous rnd and first 2 sts of this rnd), reposition marker before dcd, yo, *dcd, yo, k1, yo; rep from * to last 3 sts, dcd, yo—52 sts rem.
Rnd 5 (Dec Rnd): Dcd (last st of previous rnd and first 2 sts of this rnd), reposition marker before dcd, k1, *yo, dcd, yo, k1; rep from * to end of rnd—50 sts rem.
Rnd 7 (Dec Rnd): Dcd (last st of previous rnd and first 2 sts of this rnd), reposition marker before dcd, yo, *dcd, yo, k1, yo; rep from * to last 3 sts, dcd, yo—48 sts rem.
Rnd 9 (Dec Rnd): Dcd (last st of previous rnd and first 2 sts of this rnd), reposition marker before dcd, k1, *yo, dcd, yo, k1; rep from * to end of rnd—46 sts rem.

Rnds 2, 4, 6, and 8: Knit to last st. Do not knit last st.
Rnd 3 (Dec Rnd): Dcd (last st of previous rnd and first 2 sts of this rnd), reposition marker before dcd, yo, *dcd, yo, k1, yo; rep from * to last 3 sts, dcd, yo—60 sts rem.
Rnd 5 (Dec Rnd): Dcd (last st of previous rnd and first 2 sts of this rnd), reposition marker before dcd, k1, *yo, dcd, yo, k1; rep from * to end of rnd—58 sts rem.
Rnd 7 (Dec Rnd): Dcd (last st of previous rnd and first 2 sts of this rnd), reposition marker before dcd,

yo, *dcd, yo, k1, yo; rep from * to last 3 sts, dcd, yo—56 sts rem.
Rnd 9: Dcd (last st of previous rnd and first 2 sts of this rnd), reposition marker before dcd, yo, k1, yo, *dcd, yo, k1, yo; rep from * to end of rnd.
Rnds 10, 12, and 14: Knit.
Rnd 11: *Yo, k1, yo, dcd; rep from * to end of rnd.
Rnd 13: *Yo, dcd, yo, k1; rep from * to end of rnd.
Rnd 15: K1, *yo, k1, yo, dcd; rep from * to last 2 sts, dcd (last 2 sts of rnd and first st of next rnd).

Rnd 11 (Dec Rnd): Dcd (last st of previous rnd and first 2 sts of this rnd), reposition marker before dcd, yo, *dcd, yo, k1, yo; rep from * to last 3 sts, dcd, yo—44 sts rem.

Rnd 13 (Dec Rnd): Dcd (last st of previous rnd and first 2 sts of this rnd), reposition marker before dcd, k1, *yo, dcd, yo, k1; rep from * to end of rnd—42 sts rem.

Rnd 15 (Dec Rnd): Dcd (last st of previous rnd and first 2 sts of this rnd), reposition marker before dcd, yo, *dcd, yo, k1, yo; rep from * to last 3 sts, dcd, yo—40 sts rem.

Rnd 17 (Dec Rnd): Dcd (last st of previous rnd and first 2 sts of this rnd), reposition marker before dcd, k1, *yo, dcd, yo, k1; rep from * to end of rnd—38 sts rem.

Rnd 19 (Dec Rnd): Dcd (last st of previous rnd and first 2 sts of this rnd), reposition marker before dcd, yo, *dcd, yo, k1, yo; rep from * to last 3 sts, dcd, yo—36 sts rem.

Rnd 21: Dcd (last st of previous rnd and first 2 sts of this rnd), reposition marker before dcd, yo, k1, yo, *dcd, yo, k1, yo; rep from * to end of rnd.

Rnds 22, 24, and 26: Knit.

Rnd 23: *Yo, k1, yo, dcd; rep from * to end of rnd.

Rnd 25: *Yo, dcd, yo, k1; rep from * to end of rnd.

Rnd 27: K1, *yo, k1, yo, dcd; rep from * to last 2 sts, dcd (last 2 sts of this rnd and first st of next rnd); reposition marker after dcd.

Rnd 28: Knit.

Rep Rnds 25–28 until piece measures 21" (53.5 cm) from CO edge, ending with Rnd 28.

Heel

Note: You will be working the heel back and forth in short rows (see page 151). The st marker remains in place to mark center of heel now, rather than beginning of row.

Setup Row 1: K10, transfer rem 2 sts to Needle 2.

Setup Row 2: Turn, p18, transfer rem 4 sts to Needle 3.

Row 1: Knit to last st, wrap st, turn work.

Row 2: Purl to last st, wrap st, turn work.

Rows 3–14: Rep Rows 1 and 2; you should have placed 7 sts on hold on each side of heel.

Row 15: Knit to first wrapped st, k2tog (wrap and wrapped st), turn work.

Row 16: Purl to first wrapped st, p2tog (wrap and wrapped st), turn work.

Rows 17–28: Rep Rows 3 and 4; you should have reactivated all wrapped sts.

Foot

Change to working in the round. You should have 18 sts on Needle 1 for foot, and 9 sts each on Needles 2 and 3 for instep.

Rnd 1: K18, k2, *yo, dcd, yo, k1; rep from * to end of rnd.

Rnd 2: Knit.

Rnd 3: K18, *yo, dcd, yo, k1; rep from * to last 2 sts, k2.

Rnd 4: Knit.

Rep Rnds 1–4 until foot measures 7" (18 cm) from beg of short-row shaping or 2" (5 cm) less than desired length, ending with rnd 4.

Toe

Rnd 1: K1, ssk, knit to last 3 sts on Needle 1, k2tog, k2, ssk, knit to last 3 sts on Needle 3, k2tog, k1—32 sts rem.

Rnd 2: Knit.

Rep Rnds 1 and 2 six times—8 sts rem. Transfer first 4 sts to Needle 1 and last 4 sts to Needle 2. With 3-Needle BO (see page 156), BO all sts. Weave in all ends to WS and secure.

Make second stocking to match first.

Champagne Drinks

Bubbly Baubles

It's all in the details. Whether its beads, bobbles, or surface work, taking the time to add embellishments transforms an ordinary knitted piece into something extraordinary.

Beads can be added to knitting in many different ways. We chose to keep it simple for our projects in this chapter, so you can get your feet wet. You may typically think of a bead as having a hole in the middle and having a tubelike shape. We've changed it up a bit by using donuts. They still have a hole in the middle, but they're flattened. The "chain" of the necklace and earrings is knitted as well. So, instead of knitting a piece and stringing it onto some type of jewelry cord, we've made the cord—and combined yarns for a glittering effect.

Here's how to work the I-Cord: With a double-pointed or circular needle, cast on the number of stitches specified in the pattern. Without turning your needle, °slide stitches to the opposite end of the

needle. The working yarn will be at the stitch on the far side of the needle. Pull the working yarn firmly and knit the first stitch of the next row. Continue knitting across°. Repeat from ° to °.

The Lark's Head Knot that is used to attach the donut to the knitted tube is the same technique as for attaching fringe. But for fringe, you would use cut strands of yarn instead of a knitted tube.

In knitting, the terms "popcorn" and "bobble" are often used interchangeably. But they are different. Popcorns are generally a bit smaller than bobbles, and you do not turn and work back and forth on the popcorn stitches. A bobble is a type of texture created on the surface of the knitted fabric. To create a bobble, increase in a stitch, work a few rows on those stitches, and then decrease back to one stitch. Try out some of our favorite variations, shown on the following pages.

POPCORN

Create subtle texture.

(K1, p1, k1, p1, k1) in one st.
Sl second, third, fourth, and fifth sts over first st—1 st rem.

BOBBLE VARIATION 1

Make bobbles separately, then attach.

CO 1 st.
[Kf&b twice, k1] in same st—5 sts.
Knit 1 row. Purl 1 row.
Rep from * to * once.
K2tog, k1, k2tog—3 sts rem.
Sp2p—1 st rem.
 Fasten off. Double knot the CO and fasten off tails to create a bobble. Use these tails to attach the bobble to anything you like.

BOBBLE VARIATION 2

Insert a bobble while knitting.

Step 1

[Kf&b twice, k1] in same st—5 sts.

Step 2

[Turn, p5, turn, k5] twice.

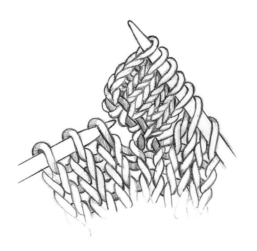

Step 3

Slip second, third, fourth, and fifth sts over first st—1 st rem.
Knit the final st to secure bobble.

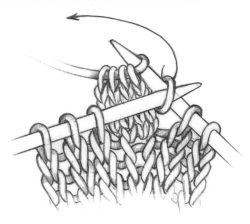

PLAID

Embroider vertical stripes.

Use Duplicate stitch (also known as Swiss darning) to create a more masculine embellishment: handsome plaids. Once you have finished knitting the project, follow the illustration below to embroider vertical lines onto the garment, mimicking the effect of plaid. No one but you needs to know how easy it is!

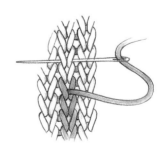

Blue Fizz Men's Plaid Hat

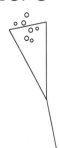

It looks hard, but it isn't! The complex colorwork of this plaid hat is achieved through simple stripes, accented with duplicate stitch embroidery. Make one for yourself, or treat that special someone.

REFRESH
Knitting in the Round
(page 37)
Duplicate Stitch (page 54)

Finished Size
Small (Medium, Large)
Circumference: 20 (21¾, 23½)" [51 (55, 59.5) cm]
Size shown: Medium

Ingredients
75 (81, 87) yds [68.5 (74, 79.5) m] lightweight alpaca yarn in light blue (MC) **3**

40 (43, 48) yds [36.5 (39.5, 44) m] lightweight alpaca yarn in natural (A) **3**

21 (24, 29) yds [19 (22, 26.5) m] lightweight alpaca yarn in medium blue (B) **3**

15 (17, 18) yds [13.5 (15.5, 16.5) m] lightweight alpaca yarn in dark blue (C) **3**

Set of five size 4 (3.5mm) double-pointed knitting needles (dpn), or size to obtain gauge

Stitch marker

Tapestry needle

Shown: Alpaca with a Twist Baby Twist (100% alpaca; 110 yds [100 m] per 50 g ball): #1004 Cloudy Sky (MC), #0100 Natural (A), #1008 Blue Corn (B), #1006 Nautical Blue (C), 1 ball each

Gauge
22 sts and 29 rows = 4" (10 cm) in Stockinette stitch (St st)
Don't free-pour; do a gauge swatch!

Stitch Explanation
2 × 2 Rib (multiple of 4 sts):
All Rnds: *K2, p2; rep from * to end of rnd.

Stripe Sequence: *Work 6 rnds in MC, 2 rnds in A, 4 rnds in B, 2 rnds in A. Rep from * for Stripe Sequence.

Begin Hat

With MC, CO 108 (120, 128) sts and divide sts onto 4 dpn [27 (30, 32) sts on each needle]. Join sts into a circle, being careful not to twist CO edge; place marker (pm) for beg of rnd. Beg 2 × 2 Rib. Work even until piece measures 2" (5 cm) from CO edge.

Change to St st and Stripe Sequence, inc 2 (0, 2) sts evenly spaced on first rnd—110 (120, 130) sts. Work even until piece measures 6½ (7, 7½)" [16.5 (18, 19) cm] from CO edge, or to desired length.

Shape Hat

Rnd 1: Continuing with Stripe Sequence as established, *k8, k2tog; rep from * to end of rnd—99 (108, 117) sts rem.

Rnd 2: *K7, k2tog; rep from * to end of rnd—88 (96, 104) sts rem.
Rnd 3: *K6, k2tog; rep from * to end of rnd—77 (84, 91) sts rem.
Rnd 4: *K5, k2tog; rep from * to end of rnd—66 (72, 78) sts rem.
Rnd 5: *K4, k2tog; rep from * to end of rnd—55 (60, 65) sts rem.
Rnd 6: *K3, k2tog; rep from * to end of rnd—44 (48, 52) sts rem.
Rnd 7: *K2, k2tog; rep from * to end of rnd—33 (36, 39) sts rem.
Rnd 8: *K1, k2tog; rep from * to end of rnd—22 (24, 26) sts rem.
Rnd 9: *K2tog; rep from * to end of rnd—11 (12, 13) sts rem.

Finishing

Cut yarn, leaving 6" (15 cm) tail. Thread tapestry needle with tail and insert through rem sts. Pull to tighten.

Cut 11 (12, 13) 50" (127 cm) lengths each of A and C. Starting with first st of first rnd of hat after ribbing, count to fifth st. *With one length of C, work vertical column of duplicate st, end where st is decreased in a k2tog. Cut yarn, leaving a 6" (15 cm) tail. Count to fifth st to the left of this column. With one length of A, work vertical column of duplicate st to top of hat, following decs. Count to fifth st to the left of this column. Rep from * until you have 22 (24, 26) Duplicate st columns, 11 (12, 13) each of A and C. Weave in all ends to WS and secure.

Flirtini Necklace and Earrings Set

Elegant effervescence can be yours! Who knew an I-Cord could look like this? Gemstone donuts and sterling findings add the finishing touches to this "tickle you pink" set. Go for a different look by easily changing out the donut pendant. Make the cord longer or shorter to fit your taste.

Finished Size

Necklace: ⅛" (3.3 mm) wide × 23" (58.5 cm) long, not including clasp
Earrings: 1¼" (3 cm) long, not including earring wires

Ingredients

40 yds (36.5 m) metallic filament

40 yds (36.5 m) super fine–weight mohair/silk blend yarn **1**

One pair size 0 (2 mm) double-pointed needles (dpn)

Flexible beading needle

1 (30 mm) rose quartz donut

2 (15 mm) rose quartz donuts

1 silver hook and ring clasp

2 silver earring wires

Jeweler's glue

Shown: South West Trading Company Slimmer Shimmer (50% nylon, 50% polyester; 350 yds [320 m] per 25 g cone): #406 Imperial (A) is the glitz, 1 cone; and Cascade Yarns Madil Yarns Kid Seta (70% kid mohair, 30% silk; 230 yds [210 m] per 25 g ball): #463 (B) is the fizz, 1 ball

Gauge

Not essential for necklace and earrings

59

Necklace

With one strand each of A and B held together, CO 3 sts. Beg I-Cord (see page 53). Work even until piece measures 26" (66 cm) from CO edge. BO all sts.

Finishing

Attach one half of jewelry clasp to necklace by pulling CO tail through the jump ring and tying a square knot. Rep for second half of jewelry clasp and BO tail. Weave in ends to inside of I-Cord. Apply jeweler's glue to cut ends.

Step 1

Fold I-Cord in half. Insert loop through hole in donut as illustrated.

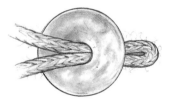

Step 2

Pull ends with attached clasps through loop and tighten to secure donut. Take care when tightening to make sure that both cords are the same length.

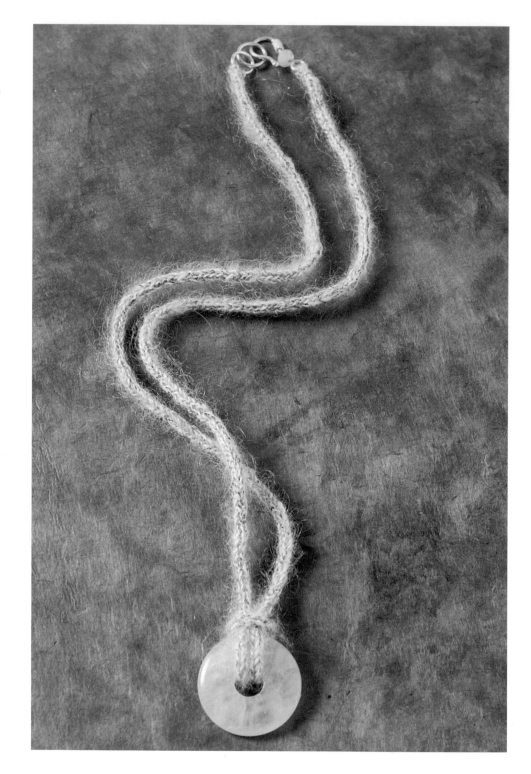

Earrings (make 2)

With one strand each of A and B held together, CO 3 sts. Beg I-Cord. Work even until piece measures 2" (5 cm) from CO edge. BO all sts.

Finishing

Slide one small donut onto I-Cord. Knot tails from CO and BO ends to form a circle.

Using flexible beading needle, pull yarn tails through loop at base of earring wire as illustrated and tie square knot. Weave in ends to inside of I-Cord. Apply jeweler's glue to cut ends. Repeat finishing instructions for second earring.

Frozen Fruit Daiquiri Necklace

Shake things up with this unusual necklace. Start off with easy I-Cord, then knit into the side of it to create scallops. Use a fabulous silk yarn that will do all the hard work for you; it already has the sequins attached! Add a handcrafted glass pendant and let your needles do the mambo!

Finished Size

20" (51 cm) long

Ingredients

35 yds (32 m) medium-weight silk sequinned yarn **4**

One size 3 (3.25 mm) 16" (40.5 cm) circular (circ) knitting needle, or size to obtain gauge

Glass pendant

Gold hook-and-eye jewelry clasp

Tapestry needle

Jeweler's glue

Shown: Tilli Tomas Disco Lights (100% spun silk with sequins; 225 yds [205.5 m] per 100 g hank): Coral Sap, 1 hank; Fire Mountain Gems gold hook and eye clasp; Hamilton Fhiber and Glass handcrafted glass pendant

Gauge

Not essential for necklace

Begin Necklace

CO 3 sts. Begin I-Cord (see page 53). Work even for 163 rnds (piece should measure approximately 20" [51 cm] long). BO all sts.

Add Scalloped BO

Turn I-Cord sideways and working into the second st from each round, pick up and knit 163 sts.

Row 1: BO 8, k3 (4 sts rem on right-hand needle), turn.
Row 2: P4, turn.
Row 3: BO 11, k3, turn.
Row 4: P4, turn.
Rows 5–8: Rep Rows 3 and 4.
Row 9: BO 11, k3, turn.
Row 10: P4, turn.
Row 11: K4, turn.
Row 12: P4, turn.
Rows 13–32: Rep Rows 9–12.
Rows 33–40: Rep Rows 3 and 4.
BO rem sts.

Make Bail

CO 6 sts.

Row 1: Purl.

Row 2: Knit.

Rows 3–10: Rep Rows 1 and 2.

BO all sts purlwise.

Finishing

Wrap bail around necklace between the 2 center scallops and sew CO and BO edges together. Whip stitch metal bail on pendant to back of knitted bail. Using beg and ending tails of necklace, attach jewelry clasp to each end of necklace. Weave in all ends to WS and secure. Apply jeweler's glue to cut ends.

Tip

- To prevent headaches when weaving in the ends, carefully cut sequins off of their thread before weaving in the ends or sewing with the yarn.

Disco Fizz Purse

Get ready to boogie to the beat with an accessory that's outta sight. Your own glittering disco . . . purse! Take it to the max and totally cover it with bobbles or space them apart for a far-out look. Some of the bobbles are created as you knit the foundation fabric. Then, the purse is embellished with more bobbles in groovy metallics. Sweet!

Finished Size

11" (28 cm) wide at base × 7¾" (19.5 cm) high, not including handles

Ingredients

210 yds (192 m) medium-weight wool yarn in blue (MC) (4)

50 yds (45 m) medium weight cotton/nylon/polyester blend yarn in blue/green metallics (A) (4)

175 yds (160 m) lightweight nylon/lamé-blend yarn in pastel metallics (B) (3)

One pair size 4 (3.5 mm) straight knitting needles, or size to obtain gauge

1 pair clear acrylic purse handles, 6" (15 cm) wide at base

1 sheet plastic needlepoint canvas or piece of cardboard (optional)

Tapestry needle

Shown: Plymouth Yarn Galway (100% pure wool; 210 yds [192 m] per 100 g ball): #139 (MC), 1 ball; Plymouth Yarn Magnum (42% rayon, 24% acrylic, 23% cotton, 9% nylon, 2% polyester; 50 yds [45.5 m] per 50 g ball): #2097 (A), 1 ball; Plymouth Yarn 24K (82% nylon, 18% lamé; 187 yds [171 m] per 50 g ball): #987 (B), 1 ball; Prym-Dritz Corporation purse handles

Gauge

22 sts and 32 rows = 4" (10 cm) in Stockinette stitch (St st)
Don't free-pour; do a gauge swatch!

65

Stitch Explanation

MB: Follow instructions at beg of chapter for Bobble Variation 2, Insert a Bobble while Knitting (see page 54)

Note

Remember that inc 1-P is worked slightly differently when you're on a purl row (see page 153).

Front and Back (both alike)

Note: Front and back are worked from the top down.
With MC, CO 45 sts.
Rows 1, 5, 9, 17, 23, 27, 29, 31, 51, 55, 59, and 61: Knit.
Rows 2, 4, 6, 8, 10, 12, 16, 18, 20, 22, 24, 26, 30, 32, 34, 36, 38, 40, 44, 46, 48, 50, 52, 54, 58, and 60: Purl.
Row 3: K9, mb, k25, mb, k9.
Row 7: K1, inc 1, k16, mb, k26, inc 1, k1—47 sts.

Row 11: K30, mb, k16.
Row 13: K3, mb, k43.
Row 14: P1, inc 1-P, purl to last st, inc 1-P, p1—49 sts.
Row 15: Knit to last 5 sts, mb, k4.
Row 19: K16, mb, knit to end.
Row 21: K1, inc 1, knit to last st, inc 1, k1—51 sts.
Row 25: K6, mb, K26, mb, knit to end of row.
Row 28: P1, inc 1-P, purl to last st, inc 1-P, p1—53 sts.
Row 33: K16, mb, K26, mb, knit to end of row.
Row 35: K1, inc 1, knit to last st, inc 1, k1—55 sts.
Row 37: K4, mb, knit to end of row.
Row 39: K29, mb, knit to end of row.
Row 41: K12, mb, knit to end of row.
Row 42: P1, inc 1-P, purl to last st, inc 1-P, p1—57 sts.
Row 43: K39, mb, knit to end of row.
Row 45: Knit to last 5 sts, mb, k4.
Row 47: K23, mb, knit to end of row.
Row 49: K1, inc 1, k2, mb, knit to last st, inc 1, k1—59 sts.
Row 53: Knit to last 15 sts, mb, knit to end of row.
Row 56: P1, inc 1-P, purl to last st, inc 1-P, p1—61 sts.

Row 57: K19, mb, knit to last 5 sts, mb, knit to end of row.
Row 62: Purl.
BO all sts.

Side Panel (make 2)

With MC, CO 11 sts. Beg St st. Work even until piece measures 7¾" (19.5 cm) from CO edge, ending with a WS row. BO all sts.

Base

With MC, CO 11 sts. Beg St st. Work even until piece measures 11" (28 cm) from CO edge, ending with a WS row. BO all sts.

Finishing

Steam block all pieces. With RS's facing, using Mattress St (see page 156), sew side edge of one side panel to side edge of front. Sew second side panel to opposite edge of front. Rep for one side of back.

Top Edging

RS facing, with A, pick up and knit 1 st in each st along top edge of pieces. *Note: Top edge of front and back is the narrower CO edge; bottom edge is the wider BO edge.* Knit 3 rows. Purl 1 row. Knit 1 row. Purl 1 row. BO all sts. Fold edging to inside of purse and sew BO edge to pickup row, being careful not to let sts show on RS. Sew rem back and side panel seam and edging seam. Sew base to BO edges of pieces.

Attach Handles

With A, sew each end of one handle to top edging, making sure handle is in center of piece.

Make Separate Bobbles

With B, make 15 bobbles (or desired number), following instructions for Bobble Variation 1 on page 54.
With A, make 14 bobbles (or desired number), as follows:
CO 1 st.
[Kf&b, k1] in same st—3 sts. Knit 1 row. Purl 1 row.
Pass second and third sts over first st—1 st rem. Fasten off.

Double knot CO and BO tails together. Thread tails through sts in desired location on front or back, making sure to keep a full or half st between the tails. Tie double knot on WS and trim ends. Space out bobbles as desired. *Note: You might want to place all the bobbles first, then knot them when you are satisfied with their location.*

Bottom Liner (optional)

For added stability, cut a 2" (5 cm) × 11" (28 cm) rectangle of plastic needlepoint canvas or cardboard, and place in bottom of purse.

Tropical Drinks

THE KNITTER'S GUIDE TO *YARN COCKTAILS*

Sweet and Sour: Sharp Angles and Soft Edges

Mitering usually makes you think of woodworking: precise angles created by sharp instruments. The symmetry of a picture frame is very soothing, all those lovely 45 degree angles fitting perfectly in the sweet spot just where they should be. Soothing, but not exciting. Mitered knitting has an element of mystery and excitement to it that is positively exhilarating. By double-decreasing in the same spot in the middle of your knitting, you are shaping an angle. Do this every other row and you will create a 90 degree angle of your own, resulting in a square or a triangle, or even an L shape. Once you have completed your first unit, pick up stitches to make another, and then another. The juxtaposition of precise angles and soft fabric is like sweet-and-sour sauce; it brings all the ingredients together in perfect harmony. Add different yarns and different colors, and let your imagination run free!

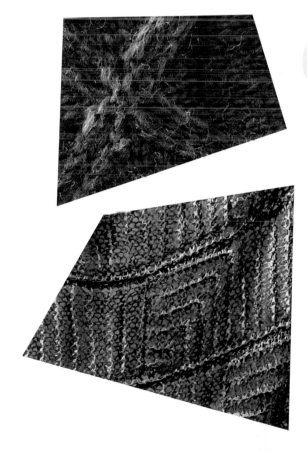

Cuba Libre Necktie

Knot just another necktie! The perfect complement to his power suit, this necktie pulls the outfit together in more ways than one. A series of mitered squares are stacked on top of each other. The squares gradually decrease to taper to the neck for ease and comfort. Two fabulous yarns, a hand-dyed silk and a hand-dyed rayon, combine in textured stripes to create a wearable work of art for your CEO.

REFRESH
Textures (page 23)

Finished Size
2½" (6.5 cm) wide at widest point × 52½" (133.5 cm) long

Ingredients
90 yds (82 m) fine-weight rayon yarn in multicolor browns and greens (MC)

63 yds (57.5 m) fine-weight 100% silk yarn in greenish gold (A)

One pair size 1 (2.25 mm) straight knitting needles, or size to obtain gauge

One size 1 (2.25 mm) 32" (81.5 cm) -long circular (circ) knitting needle

Stitch holder

Tapestry needle

Shown: Blue Heron Yarns Softwist Rayon (100% rayon; 590 yds [539.5 m] per 264 g hank): Kelp (MC), 1 hank; Fiesta Yarns La Luz (100% spun mulberry silk; 220 yds [201 m] per 2 oz hank): Pinon (A), 1 hank

Gauge
24 sts and 14 rows = 4" (10 cm) in Garter St with MC
Don't free-pour; do a gauge swatch!

Tips

- Double-pointed needles were used to make the necktie shown and work the 3-Needle BO. Circular needles were used to pick up and knit sts for the edging.

- Remember that this necktie is going to stretch vertically when worn; make sure your gauge matches or the tie will be very droopy.

- If you're having a hard time with the double centered decrease, go ahead and work a k3tog instead. Either will decrease the correct number of stitches; the difference is that the k3tog slants to the right, whereas the double centered decrease does not slant.

Stitch Explanation

Dcd (double centered decrease): Sl 2 sts together knitwise as if to k2tog, k1, pass 2 slipped sts over—2 sts decreased.

Stripe Sequence: *Work in A for 2 rows, then MC for 2 rows; rep from * for Stripe Sequence.

Note

The first st of every row will be slipped purlwise, to create a selvedge.

Front

Square 1

With MC, CO 31 sts. Sl 1, knit to end of row.

Row 1 (RS): Begin Stripe Sequence. Sl 1, k13, dcd, knit to end of row—29 sts rem.

Rows 2, 6, 10, 14, 18, 22, and 26: Sl 1, purl to last st, k1.

Row 3: Sl 1, k12, dcd, knit to end of row—27 sts rem.

Rows 4, 8, 12, 16, 20, and 24: Sl 1, knit to end of row.

Row 5: Sl 1, k11, dcd, knit to end of row—25 sts rem.

Row 7: Sl 1, k10, dcd, knit to end of row—23 sts rem.

Row 9: Sl 1, k9, dcd, knit to end of row—21 sts rem.

Row 11: Sl 1, k8, dcd, knit to end of row—19 sts rem.

Row 13: Sl 1, k7, dcd, knit to end of row—17 sts rem.

Row 15: Sl 1, k6, dcd, knit to end of row—15 sts rem.

Row 17: Sl 1, k5, dcd, knit to end of row—13 sts rem.

Row 19: Sl 1, k4, dcd, knit to end of row—11 sts rem.

Row 21: Sl 1, k3, dcd, knit to end of row—9 sts rem.

Row 23: Sl 1, k2, dcd, knit to end of row—7 sts rem.

Row 25: Sl 1, k1, dcd, knit to end of row—5 sts rem.

Row 27: Sl 1, dcd, k1—3 sts rem.

Row 28: K3tog—1 st rem. Fasten off, but do not cut yarns.

Square 2

RS facing, continuing with same strand of MC, pick up and knit 16 sts from right to left along left shaping edge of square just completed (see Assembly Diagram).

Row 1 (WS): Sl 1, knit to end of row.

Row 2: Rep Row 1.

Row 3: With Cable CO (see page 149), CO 15 sts, knit back across these sts, then knit to end of row—31 sts. Work Rows 1–28 of Square 1.

Squares 3, 4, and 5

Work as for Square 2.

Square 6 (Dec Square)

RS facing, continuing with same strand of MC, pick up and knit 16 sts from right to left along left shaping edge of square just completed.

Row 1 (WS): Sl 1, k2tog, knit to last 3 sts, k2tog, k1—14 sts rem.

Row 2: Sl 1, knit to end of row.

Row 3: With Cable CO, CO 13 sts, knit back across these sts, then knit to end of row—27 sts total. Work Rows 5–28 of Square 1.

Square 7 (Dec Square)

RS facing, continuing with same strand of MC, pick up and knit 14 sts from right to left along left shaping edge of square just completed.

Row 1 (WS): Sl 1, k2tog, knit to last 3 sts, k2tog, k1—12 sts rem.

Row 2: Sl 1, knit to end of row.

Row 3: With Cable CO, CO 11 sts, knit back across these sts, then knit to end of row—23 sts total. Work Rows 9–28 of Square 1.

Square 8 (Dec Square)

RS facing, continuing with same strand of MC, pick up and knit 12 sts from right to left along left shaping edge of square just completed.

Row 1 (WS): Sl 1, k2tog, knit to last 3 sts, k2tog, k1—10 sts rem.

Row 2: Sl 1, knit to end of row.

Row 3: With Cable CO, CO 9 sts, knit back across these sts, then knit to end of row—19 sts total. Work Rows 13–28 of Square 1.

Square 9 (Dec Square)

RS facing, continuing with same strand of MC, pick up and knit 10 sts from right to left along left shaping edge of square just completed.

Row 1 (WS): Sl 1, k2tog, knit to last 3 sts, k2tog, k1—8 sts rem.

Row 2: Sl 1, knit to end of row.

Row 3: With Cable CO, CO 7 sts, knit back across these sts, then knit to end of row—15 sts total. Work Rows 17–28 of Square 1.

Square 10

RS facing, continuing with same strand of MC, pick up and knit 8 sts from right to left along left shaping edge of square just completed.

Row 1 (WS): Sl 1, knit to end of row.

Row 2: Rep Row 1.

Row 3: With Cable CO, CO 7 sts, knit back across these sts, then knit to end of row—15 sts total. Work Rows 17–28 of Square 1.

Squares 11–13

Work as for Square 10.

RS facing, continuing with same strand of MC, pick up and knit 8 sts from right to left along left shaping edge of square just completed. Sl 1, knit to end of row. Place sts on holder for 3-Needle BO.

Back

Square 14

With MC, CO 27 sts. Sl 1, knit to end of row.

Beg Stripe Sequence. Work Rows 5–28 of Square 1.

Square 15

RS facing, continuing with same strand of MC, pick up and knit 14 sts from right to left along left shaping edge of square just completed.

Row 1 (WS): Sl 1, knit to end of row.

Row 2: Rep Row 1.

Row 3: With Cable CO, CO 13 sts, knit back across these sts, then knit to end of row—27 sts total. Beg Stripe Sequence. Work Rows 5–28 of Square 1.

Squares 16 and 17

Work as for Square 15.

Square 18 (Dec Square)

Work as for Square 7.

Square 19 (Dec Square)

Work as for Square 8.

Square 20 (Dec Square)

Work as for Square 9.

Squares 21–24

Work as for Square 10.

RS facing, continuing with same strand of MC, pick up and knit 8 sts from right to left along left shaping edge of square just completed. Sl 1, knit to end of row. Leave sts on needle for 3-Needle BO.

Finishing

Transfer sts from front holder to needle. With 3-Needle BO (see page 156), BO front and back sts.

Edging: RS facing, beg at right edge of CO row of Square 1, with MC, pick up and knit 1 st in CO row, 1 st in each selvedge st and 1 st in each pickup row between squares along right edge of necktie, then 1 st in 3-Needle BO—158 sts. BO all sts knitwise. Rep for back of tie, beg at right edge of CO row of Square 14—120 sts. BO all sts knitwise. Weave in all ends to WS and secure. Lightly mist with water and block to measurements if desired.

ASSEMBLY DIAGRAM

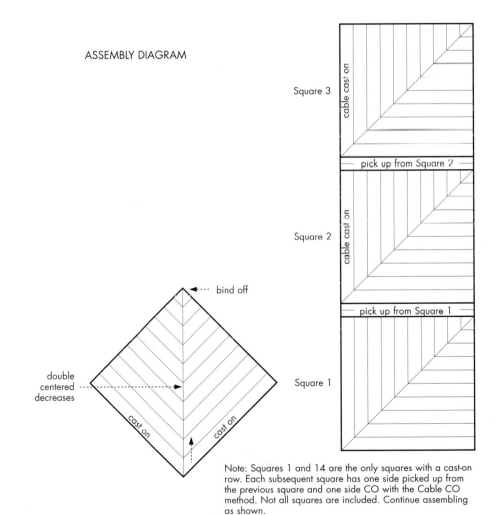

Note: Squares 1 and 14 are the only squares with a cast-on row. Each subsequent square has one side picked up from the previous square and one side CO with the Cable CO method. Not all squares are included. Continue assembling as shown.

Blue Bayou Mitered Stole

*This gorgeous stole gives new meaning to the phrase "the Big Easy."
Five strips alternate mitered squares with simple striped squares. Join them
together with 3-Needle BO, and you are ready to go. A shimmery rayon
ribbon and a fluffy mohair provide textural contrast, mirroring the deep
blue of the bayou. Laissez les bon temps rouler!*

REFRESH
Textures (page 23)

Finished Size

Approximately 62" (157.5 cm) long ×
29" (73.5 cm) wide
Note: This stole is very stretchy, so
measurements will vary slightly.

Ingredients

668 yds (611 m) ⅛" [3 mm] -wide
medium-weight 100% rayon hand-
dyed ribbon yarn in blues (MC) **4**

272 yds (248.5 m) medium-weight
100% brushed kid mohair yarn in
blues (A) **4**

One pair size 10½ (6.5 mm) straight
knitting needles, or size to obtain
gauge

Two size 10½ (6.5 mm) 29" (73.5 cm)
-long circular (circ) knitting needles

Tapestry needle

Point protectors (optional)

Shown: Fiesta Yarns Gelato (100%
rayon; 262 yds [239.5 m] per 3 oz
hank): #3104 Alaska (MC), 3 hanks;
Fiesta Yarns Heaven (100% brushed
kid mohair; 260 yds [237.5 m] per
2 oz [57 g] hank): #8104 Alaska (A),
2 hanks

Gauge

20 sts and 30 rows = 4" (10 cm) in
Garter St (knit every row) with MC
Don't free-pour; do a gauge swatch!

Stitch Explanation

Stripe Sequence: *Work in A for 2
rows, then MC for 2 rows; rep from
* for Stripe Sequence.

Note

The first st of every row will be slipped purlwise, to create a selvedge.

Strip 1

Square 1 (Mitered Square)

With MC, CO 25 sts. Sl 1, knit to end of row.

Row 1 (RS): Beg Stripe Sequence. Sl 1, k10, k3tog, knit to end of row—23 sts rem.

Rows 2, 6, 10, 14, and 18: Sl 1, purl to last st, k1.

Row 3: Sl 1, k9, k3tog, knit to end of row—21 sts rem.

Rows 4, 8, 12, 16, and 20: Sl 1, knit to end of row.

Row 5: Sl 1, k8, k3tog, knit to end of row—19 sts rem.

Row 7: Sl 1, k7, k3tog, knit to end of row—17 sts rem.

Row 9: Sl 1, k6, k3tog, knit to end of row—15 sts rem.

Row 11: Sl 1, k5, k3tog, knit to end of row—13 sts rem.

Row 13: Sl 1, k4, k3tog, knit to end of row—11 sts rem.

Row 15: Sl 1, k3, k3tog, knit to end of row—9 sts rem.

Row 17: Sl 1, k2, k3tog, knit to end of row—7 sts rem.

Row 19: Sl 1, k1, k3tog, knit to end of row—5 sts rem.

Row 21: Sl 1, k3tog, k1—3 sts rem.

Row 22: K3tog—1 st rem. Do not cut yarn.

Square 2 (Striped Square)

RS facing, continuing with same strand of MC, k1 (last st from Mitered Square), pick up and knit 12 sts from right to left along left shaping edge of Mitered Square just completed (see Assembly Diagram) —13 sts. Sl 1, knit to end.
Row 1 (RS): Beg Stripe Sequence. Sl 1, knit to end of row.
Rows 2, 6, 10, 14, and 18: Sl 1, purl to last st, k1.
Rows 3–5, 7–9, 11–13, and 15–17: Sl 1, knit to end of row.
Row 19: Sl 1, knit to end of row, with Cable CO (see page 149), CO 12 sts—25 sts.

Square 3 (Mitered Square)

Working on sts from row 19 of Square 2, sl 1, knit to end of row. Work Rows 1–22 of Square 1.

Rep last two squares 5 times (you should have a strip of thirteen squares, ending with Square 3). Fasten off.

Strip 2

Square 14 (Striped Square)

With MC, CO 13 sts. Sl 1, knit to end of row.
Work Rows 1–19 of Square 2.

Square 15

Work as for Square 3.

Square 16

Work as for Square 2.

Squares 17–26

Rep last two squares 5 times (you should have a strip of thirteen squares, ending with Square 2). BO all sts.

Strip 3

Work as for Strip 1.

Strip 4

Work as for Strip 2.

Strip 5

Work as for Strip 1.

Finishing

RS facing, with MC and circ needle, pick up and knit 130 sts evenly along left side of Strip 1. Knit 1 row. With second circ needle and MC, pick up and knit 130 sts evenly along right side of Strip 2. WS facing, with MC and 3-Needle BO (see page 156), BO all sts. In this same manner, attach Strips 3, 4, and 5.
Side Edging: RS facing, with MC and circ needle, pick up and knit 130 sts along left edge of stole. Knit 9 rows, slipping first st of each row. BO all sts. Rep for right edge of stole.

Tips

- As you pick up and knit sts along sides of strips in preparation for 3-Needle BO, and as you work the BO, place point protectors on the ends of the needles that are not in use, to prevent your stitches from sliding off the needles.

- When working 3-Needle BO, take your time! It will be more efficient to do it slowly and correctly the first time than to rush and have to go back and correct your mistakes.

- When picking up stitches for the edging, try to pick up into stitches that are tighter. Picking up into loose stitches will make big holes in your stole.

Top and Bottom Edging: RS facing, with MC and circ needle, pick up and knit 65 sts along top of stole, including side edging. Knit 9 rows, slipping first st of each row. BO all sts. Rep for bottom of stole. Weave in all loose ends to WS and secure. *Note: Because MC is a bit slippery, when weaving in ends, use a tapestry needle to skim yarn along tops of stitches on WS of garment to anchor the slippery ends to the fabric.* Wet-block to finished measurements if desired.

Note: The first square of each strip begins with a cast-on row. Each subsequent square is either picked up or continued from the previous square. This shows the first 5 squares of Strips 1 and 2 only.

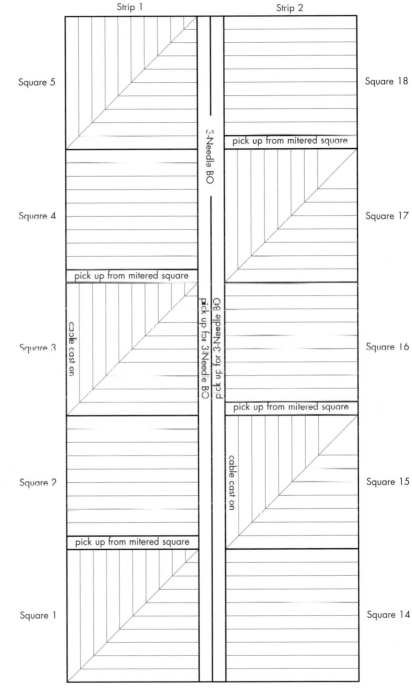

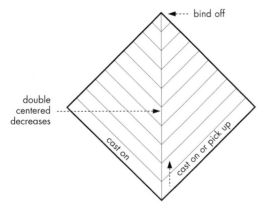

Honey Rum Swizzle Square Hat

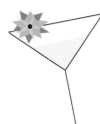

The buzz will be all about you when you knit up this unique variation of a French beret. Increases, then decreases at four corners create the mitered angles for the square top, while the bottom is hemmed for a trim, finished look. It's hip to be square!

REFRESH
Knitting in the Round
(page 37)

Finished Size
Small (Medium, Large)
Circumference: 17¼ (19½, 21¾)"
[44 (49.5, 55) cm]
Square Top: 10½ (11, 11½)" [26.5
(28, 29) cm] square
Size shown: Small

Ingredients
73 (85, 97) yds [67 (77.5, 89) m]
bulky-weight wool yarn in brown
(MC) ⑤

42 (43, 44) yds [38 (39.5, 40) m]
bulky-weight wool yarn in red (A)
⑤

20 (21, 21) yds [18 (19, 19) m]
bulky-weight wool yarn in rust (B)
⑤

Set of five size 9 (5.5 mm) double-
pointed knitting needles (dpn), or
size to obtain gauge

Stitch markers (including 1 different
color marker)

Tapestry needle

Shown: Kraemer Yarns Mauch
Chunky (100% wool; 120 yds [110
m] per 100 g ball): #Y1021 Carrot
Cake (MC), #Y1030 Rhubarb (A),
#Y1018 Spice (B), 1 ball each

Gauge
14 sts and 22 rows = 4" (10 cm) in
Stockinette stitch (St st)
Don't free pour; do a gauge swatch!

Stitch Explanation
Stripe Sequence: *Work 1 rnd in
A, 1 rnd in B, 1 rnd in A, then 3
rnds in MC; rep from * for Stripe
Sequence.

Begin Hat
With MC, CO 60 (68, 76) sts and
divide sts onto 4 dpn [15 (17, 19) sts
on each needle]. Join sts into a circle,
being careful not to twist CO edge;
place marker of different color (pm)
for beg of rnd. Knit 5 rnds. Purl 1
rnd (turning rnd). Knit 5 rnds.

79

Join Hem

Fold hem to WS at turning rnd, so that CO edge is just behind needle. *Using left-hand needle, pick up 1 st from CO edge, k2tog (picked-up st and next st on left-hand needle). Rep from * to end of rnd. Change to St st and Stripe Sequence. Work even for 9 rows.

Shape Hat

Rnd 1: Continuing in St st and Stripe Sequence as established, *k1, inc 1-R, k14 (16, 18), inc 1-L, pm; rep from * to end of rnd—68 (76, 84) sts.

Rnd 2: *K1, inc 1-R, work to next marker, inc 1-L; rep from * to end of rnd—76 (84, 92) sts. Continuing in Stripe Sequence as established, rep Rnd 2 eleven times—164 (172, 180) sts. Continuing in MC, knit 1 rnd. Purl 1 rnd (turning rnd for top of hat). Knit 1 rnd.

Mitered Decrease Section

Rnd 1: *K1, k2tog, work to 2 sts before next marker, ssk; rep from * to end of rnd—156 (164, 172) sts rem.

Beg Stripe Sequence. Rep Rnd 1 eighteen (nineteen, twenty) times—12 sts rem.

Final Decrease Rnd: *K2tog, ssk; rep from * to end of rnd—6 sts rem. Cut yarn, leaving 6" (15 cm) tail. Thread tapestry needle with tail and insert through rem sts. Pull to tighten.

Finishing

Weave in all ends to WS and secure. Lightly wet-block top of beret to square shape if needed.

Tips

- You may notice that the mitered decreases pull in, tightening your gauge at the top square of the hat a little bit. Not to worry; this is normal. If you would like, you may flip your hat upside down and wet-block the square to the square-top measurements at the beginning of the pattern.

- When changing colors for the stripes, make sure to carry yarns loosely up the back of the work. Carrying the yarns up too tightly will cause the fabric to pucker and distort.

- It is best to work your gauge swatch in the round. Many people tend to work their knit stitch a little tighter than their purl stitch. If you work your swatch flat and you knit one row, then purl the next, the row gauge will be different than if you work your swatch in the round, where you knit every row to make Stockinette stitch, and your hat won't be the right size.

Tropical Dream Camisole

This sexy camisole consists of two large mitered squares, two large mitered triangles, and two smaller triangles. The two mitered squares are knitted first. The front and the back squares are connected by picking up stitches on the sides of the squares and knitting back and forth to create mitered triangles in between. When this has been accomplished, you will have formed a tube without any knitting in the round! Complete the camisole by knitting two mitered triangles separately and sewing them to the front of the tube.

Remember that I-Cord from chapter 3? Here we are going to attach an I-Cord to stabilize the top back of the tube and form halter ties. The colors of this wonderful yarn are fresh and fruity, and the 100 percent bamboo fiber drapes beautifully to soften the mitered angles and skim the body.

REFRESH
Textures (page 23)
I-Cord (page 53)

Finished Size

Small (Medium, Large, XLarge)
To fit 30–32 (34–36, 38–40, 42–44)"
[76–81.5 (86.5–91.5, 96.5–101.5, 106.5–112.8) cm] bust
23 (26½, 30, 33½)" [58.5 (67.5, 76, 85) cm] actual chest circumference
Size shown: Medium

Ingredients

240 yds (219.5 m) medium-weight 100% bamboo yarn in light blue (MC) ❨4❩

120 yds (110 m) medium-weight 100% bamboo yarn in pink (A) ❨4❩

70 yds (64 m) medium-weight 100% bamboo yarn in orange (B) ❨4❩

One size 7 (4.5 mm) 29" (73.5 cm) -long circular knitting needle (circ), or size to obtain gauge

Two size 8 (5 mm) double-pointed knitting needles (dpn)

Tapestry needle

Shown: South West Trading Company Twizé (100% bamboo; 120 yds [110 m] per 100 g ball): #325 Twue (MC), #322 Twing (A), 2 balls each; #321 Twink (B): 1 ball

81

Gauge

20 sts and 24 rows = 4" (10 cm) in Stockinette stitch (St st) with smaller needles

Don't free-pour; do a gauge swatch!

Note

Slip all sts purlwise.

Mitered Square (make 2)

With smaller needles and MC, CO 65 (75, 85, 95) sts.

Row 1 (WS): Sl 1, knit to end of row.

Rows 2–3: Rep Row 1.

Row 4: Change to A. Sl 1, k30 (35, 40, 45), k3tog, knit to end of row—63 (73, 83, 93) sts rem.

Row 5: Sl 1, purl to last st, k1.

Row 6: Change to MC. Sl 1, k29 (34, 39, 44), k3tog, knit to end of row—61 (71, 81, 91) sts rem.

Row 7: Sl 1, knit to end of row.

Row 8: Change to A. Sl 1, k28 (33, 38, 43), k3tog, knit to end of row—59 (69, 79, 89) sts rem.

Row 9: Sl 1, purl to last st, k1.

Row 10: Change to MC. Sl 1, k27 (32, 37, 42), k3tog, knit to end of row—57 (67, 77, 87) sts rem.

Row 11: Sl 1, knit to end of row. Cont as est, working 1 less st before k3tog on each following dec row, until 33 (39, 43, 49) sts rem, ending on WS row, with MC.

Row 12 (RS): Change to B. Sl 1, k14 (17, 19, 22), k3tog, knit to end of row—31 (37, 41, 47) sts rem.

Row 13: Sl 1, knit to end of row.

Row 14: Sl 1, k13 (16, 18, 21), k3tog, knit to end of row—29 (35, 39, 45) sts rem.

Row 15: Sl 1, knit to end of row. Cont as est, working 1 less st before the dec on each following dec row, until 3 sts rem. K3tog. Fasten off.

Mitered Triangle A (Camisole Side—make 2)

Set each Mitered Square on its point to form a diamond, with section of square in B at top and side points of squares touching (see diagram on page 84). Beg just to left of point of Mitered Square, as indicated in diagram, with MC and smaller needles, pick up and knit 33 (39, 43, 49) sts down left side of one square, pick up and knit 1 st in bottom right of second square (this will become side fold line), pick up and knit 33 (37, 43, 47) sts up right side of diamond—67 (77, 87, 97) sts.

Row 1 (WS): Sl 1 st, knit to end of row.

Row 2: Change to A. Sl 1, ssk, k29 (34, 39, 44), k3tog, k29 (34, 39, 44), k2tog, k1—63 (73, 83, 93) sts rem.

Row 3: Sl 1, purl to last st, k1.

Row 4: Change to MC. Sl 1, ssk, k27 (32, 37, 42), k3tog, k27 (32, 37, 42), k2tog, k1—59 (69, 79, 89) sts rem.

Row 5: Sl 1, knit to end of row. Cont as est, working 2 less sts before and after k3tog on each following dec row, until 5 sts rem. Cut yarn, leaving a 6" (15 cm) tail. Thread tapestry needle with tail and insert through rem sts. Pull to tighten. Rep for second Mitered Triangle A, along 2 rem unattached sides of the diamonds. Complete as for first Mitered Triangle A. *(Note: When you have picked up and knit your stitches, you will have formed a tube, but you will NOT be knitting in the round.)*

Mitered Triangle B (Bodice Cups—make 2)

With MC, CO 49 (57, 65, 73) sts.

Row 1 (WS): Sl 1, knit to end of row.

Row 2: Change to A. Sl 1, ssk, k20 (24, 28, 32), k3tog, k20 (24, 28, 32), k2tog, k1—45 (53, 61, 69) sts rem.

Row 3: Sl 1, purl to last st, k1.

Row 4: Change to MC. Sl 1, ssk, k18 (22, 26, 30), k3tog, k18 (22, 26, 30), k2tog, k1—41 (49, 57, 65) sts rem.

Row 5: Sl 1, knit to end of row. Cont as est, working 2 less sts before and after k3tog on each following dec row, until 5 sts rem. Cut yarn, leaving a 6" (15 cm) tail. Thread tapestry needle with tail and insert through rem sts. Pull to tighten.

Attach Bodice Cups

With MC and tapestry needle, sew BO edge of each bodice cup to front of camisole, between fold line of Mitered Triangle A (see diagram) and point of Mitered Square, easing bodice cup if necessary.

I-Cord Ties

With MC and dpns, CO 3 sts. Work I-Cord for 32" (81.5 cm). Change to attached I-Cord as follows: K2, sl 1, pick up and knit 1 st at top point of left cup, psso. Cont as est along armhole edge of left cup, along top selvedge of back of camisole, and along armhole edge of right cup to top point of cup. Change to unattached I-Cord. Work even for 32" (81.3 cm). Fasten off.

Finishing

With Mattress st (see page 156), tapestry needle, and 6" (15 cm) of MC, sew bodice cups together along inside edges for 1" (2.5 cm). Weave in all ends to WS and secure.

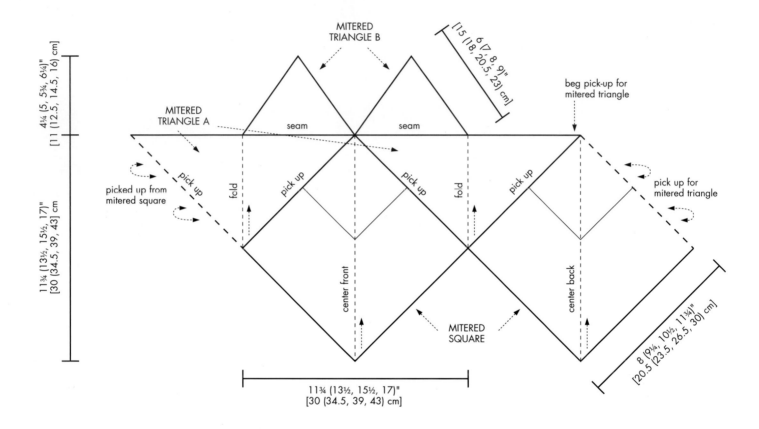

8½ (10, 11¼, 12¾)"
[21.5, 25.5, 28.5, 32.5) cm]

4¼ [5, 5¾, 6¼]"
[11 (12.5, 14.5, 16) cm]

11¾ [13½, 15½, 17]"
[30 (34.5, 39, 43] cm]

MITERED
TRIANGLE B

6 7, 8, 9]"
[15 (18, 20.5, 23] cm]

beg pick-up for
mitered triangle

MITERED
TRIANGLE A

seam

seam

picked up from
mitered square

pick up

fold

pick up

pick up

fold

pick up

pick up for
mitered triangle

center front

center back

MITERED
SQUARE

11¾ (13½, 15½, 17)"
[30 (34.5, 39, 43) cm]

8 [9¼, 10½, 11¾)"
[20.5 (23.5, 26.5, 30] cm]

84

Martini Drinks

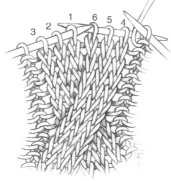

Twist and Shout!

From the simplest to the most complex, all cables employ the same technique, crossing a group of stitches over or under another group of stitches. Hold a group of stitches to the back of your work behind your needles to create a cable that slants to the right, the Back Cross Cable.

Back Cross Cable

Step 1:
Following diagram, place stitches 4, 5, and 6 on the cable needle of your choice (see Tools of the Trade, page 10) and hold to back.

Step 2:
Knit stitches 1, 2, and 3 from the left-hand needle.

Step 3:
Return to the cable needle and knit stitches 4, 5, and 6.

Front Cross Cable

Hold a group of stitches to the front of your work to create a cable that slants to the left, the Front Cross Cable.

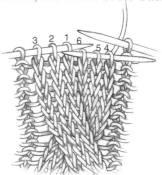

Step 1:
Following diagram, place stitches 4, 5, and 6 on the cable needle and hold to front.

Step 2:
Knit stitches 1, 2, and 3 from the left-hand needle.

Step 3:
Return to the cable needle and knit stitches 4, 5, and 6.

For some, a chart may help make the cable pattern easier to understand. An example of a chart we use is shown in the High Roller Vest (page 95).

RS rows are numbered on the right-hand side of the chart, and are read from right to left; WS rows are numbered on the left-hand side of the chart, and are read from left to right. If the pattern in the chart begins on a RS row, then the RS rows will be odd-numbered, and the WS rows will be even-numbered; if it begins on a WS row, then the WS rows will be odd-numbered, and the RS rows will be even-numbered. This numbering system ensures that you will always know whether you are working a RS or WS row, and whether you are supposed to begin on the RS or WS. Always begin the chart with Row 1. In this chart, the cable crossings occur on the odd-numbered rows and are framed by Reverse Stockinette stitch for the first 8 rows. Work the cable crossing in the stitches indicated by the symbols. For example, in Row 1, purl 6 stitches, knit 4 stitches, then purl 6 stitches. For Row 2, knit 6 stitches, purl 4 stitches, then knit 6 stitches. Note that when you are working WS rows, the chart shows what the stitch will look like on the RS. So when you see a purl symbol on a WS row, you must knit the stitch on the WS, to have a purl stitch on the RS. Rows 3 and 4 are worked in a similar manner. For Row 5, purl 4 stitches, then work C4B: Sl 2 stitches from the left-hand needle onto a cable needle and hold the cable needle at the back of your knitting, behind your needles. Knit 2 stitches from the left-hand needle. Return to the 2 sts on the cable needle and knit those 2 stitches to complete the C4B. Now, immediately work a C4F: Sl 2 stitches from the left-hand needle onto a cable needle. Hold the cable needle to the front of your knitting, in front of your needles. Knit 2 stitches from the left-hand needle. Return to the 2 stitches on the cable needle and knit those 2 stitches to complete the C4F. Purl 4 stitches to complete Row 5 of the chart. Take a deep breath, unclench your jaw, and relax. You did it!

Now that you've gotten your feet wet, mix and match cable crossings to create rope cables, double cables, and braided cables in your own unique combinations.

Dry Martini Belt

This unique belt focuses on a single cable pattern, the Oxox cable. A rectangular strip without distracting increases or decreases, this project is a great introduction to cable patterns. Linen yarn provides stability and elegance, and the belt is narrow enough to weave through belt loops. Add a handcrafted glass buckle signed by the artist and you have a functional work of art. It's a cinch!

Finished Size

Small (Medium, Large)
Fits men's waist sizes 32/34 (36/38, 40/42)" [81.5/86.5 (91.5/96.5, 101.5/106.5) cm]
2¼" (5.5 cm) wide × 40 (44, 48)" [101.5 (112, 122) cm] long actual size
Note: To adapt for women's sizes, simply work fewer repeats of pattern.
Size shown: Men's Small

Ingredients

60 (75, 90) yds [55 (68.5, 82) m] fine-weight 100% linen yarn in brown (2)

One pair size 1 (2.25 mm) straight knitting needles, or size to obtain gauge

Cable needle (cn)

Tapestry needle

1¾" (4.5 cm) square glass belt buckle with two 1⅛" (2.8 cm) -wide openings

Shown: Louet Sales Euroflax Originals (100% linen; 270 yds [247 m] per 100 g hank): #18-2024 Ginger, 1 hank; Artistic Visions Square Glass Belt Buckle, brown.

Gauge

26 sts and 40 rows = 4" (10 cm) in Stockinette stitch (St st)
Don't free-pour; do a gauge swatch!

Stitch Explanation

C4B: Sl 2 sts to cable needle and hold in back, k2, k2 from cn.
C4F: Sl 2 sts to cable needle and hold in front, k2, k2 from cn.

Note

Slip all sts purlwise.

Begin Belt

CO 12 sts.

Row 1 and all WS rows: Sl 1, k1, p8, k2.

Rows 2, 6, 10, and 14: Sl 1, p1, k8, p1, k1.

Row 4: Sl 1, p1, C4B, C4F, p1, k1.

Rows 8 and 12: Sl 1, p1, C4F, C4B, p1, k1.

Row 16: Rep Row 4.

Rep Rows 1–16 until belt measures 40 (44, 48)" [101.5 (112, 122) cm] from CO edge, ending with Row 9.

Dec Row: Sl 1, p1, *k2tog; rep from * to last 2 sts, p1, k1—8 sts rem. BO all sts knitwise. Weave in all ends to WS and secure.

Finishing

Wet-block belt to measurements. Allow to dry. Sew belt buckle to belt as follows: Insert CO end of belt up through first space of buckle, then down through second space. Fold about 1½" (4 cm) over to WS to make a loop. Whip stitch end to WS, being careful not to let sts show on RS.

After Dark Martini Sweater

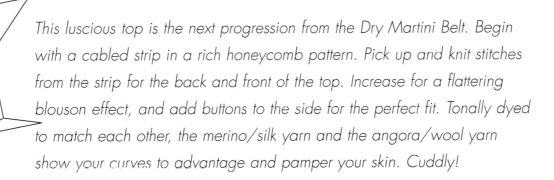

This luscious top is the next progression from the Dry Martini Belt. Begin with a cabled strip in a rich honeycomb pattern. Pick up and knit stitches from the strip for the back and front of the top. Increase for a flattering blouson effect, and add buttons to the side for the perfect fit. Tonally dyed to match each other, the merino/silk yarn and the angora/wool yarn show your curves to advantage and pamper your skin. Cuddly!

Finished Size

Small (Medium, Large, XLarge)
44 (47½, 51½, 55)" [112 (120.5, 131, 140) cm] actual chest circumference
Size shown: Medium

Ingredients

255 (280, 310, 335) yds [233 (256, 283.5, 306.5) m] medium-weight angora/wool yarn in green (MC) **4**

225 (240, 255, 270) yds [205.5 (219.5, 233, 247) m] bulky-weight merino/silk yarn in green (A) **5**

One pair size 8 (5 mm) straight knitting needles, or size to obtain gauge

One set of five size 8 (5 mm) double-pointed knitting needles (dpn), or one 16" (40.5 cm) circular (circ) knitting needle

Cable needle (cn)

Stitch holders

Stitch marker

Four ⅞" (2.2 cm) buttons

Tapestry needle

Sewing thread in matching color

Shown: Cascade Yarns Cloud Nine (50% angora, 50% wool; 109 yds [99.5 m] per 50 g ball): #111 (MC), 3 balls; Cascade Yarns Venezia (70% merino, 30% silk; 102 yds [93.5 m] per 100 g ball): #111 (A) 3 (3, 3, 4) balls

Gauge

17 sts and 28 rows = 4" (10 cm) in Stockinette stitch (St st) with MC
14 sts and 20 rows = 4" (10 cm) in Stockinette stitch (St st) with A
Don't free-pour; do a gauge swatch!

Stitch Explanation

C4B: Sl 2 sts to cn and hold in back, k2, k2 from cn.
C4F: Sl 2 sts to cn and hold in front, k2, k2 from cn.

Note

The first st of every row will be slipped purlwise, to create a selvedge.

91

Waistband

With A, CO 38 sts.

Row 1 and all WS rows: Sl 1, k2, purl to last 3 sts, k3.

Row 2: Sl 1, p2, *C4B, C4F: rep from * to last 3 sts, p2, k1.

Rows 4, 6, and 10: Sl 1, p2, knit to last 3 sts, p2, k1.

Row 8: Sl 1, p2, *C4F, C4B; rep from * to last 3 sts, p2, k1.

Row 12: Rep Row 4.

Work even until piece measures 27½ (30, 32½, 35)" [70 (76, 82.5, 89) cm] from CO edge, ending with Row 8.

Back

Fold waistband in half lengthwise and mark fold line along left edge. With MC, beg at BO edge and ending at marker, pick up and knit 36 (39, 42, 45) sts in selvedge sts along edge.

Row 1 (WS): P1, *inc 1, p1; rep from * to end of row—71 (77, 83, 89) sts.

Row 2: Knit.

Row 3: K4, *inc 1, k3; rep from * to last 4 st, inc 1, k4—93 (101, 109, 117) sts.

(RS) Beg St st. Work even until piece measures 10 (10½, 10½, 11)" [25.5 (26.5, 26.5, 28) cm] from bottom edge of waistband, ending with a WS row.

Shape Armholes (RS)

BO 4 sts at beg of next 2 rows, 2 sts at beg of next 2 rows, then dec 1 st each side every other row twice, as follows: K1, ssk, work to last 3 sts, k2tog, k1—77 (85, 93, 101) sts rem. Work even until piece measures 17 (18, 18, 19)" [43 (45.5, 45.5, 48.5) cm] from bottom edge of waistband, ending with a WS row.

Shape Neck (RS)

K19 (21, 23, 25), attach second ball of yarn, BO center 39 (43, 47, 51) sts, work to end. Using separate balls of yarn and working both sides of neckline at same time, dec 1 st each neck edge every row four times, as follows:

Row 1 (WS): On left neck edge, purl to last 3 sts, p2tog-tbl, p1; on right neck edge, p1, p2tog, purl to end of row—18 (20, 22, 24) sts rem each side.

Row 2: On right edge, knit to last 3 sts, k2tog, k1; on left edge, k1, ssk, knit to end of row—17 (19, 21, 23) sts rem each side.

Rep Rows 1 and 2 once—15 (17, 19, 21) sts rem each side. Place rem sts on holders for 3-Needle BO.

Front

With MC, beg at marker and ending at CO edge, pick up and knit 36 (39, 42, 45) sts in selvedge sts along edge. Work as for back until piece measures 14½ (15, 15, 15½)" [37 (38, 38, 39) cm] from bottom edge of waistband, ending with a WS row.

Shape Neck (RS)

K19 (21, 23, 25), attach second ball of yarn, BO center 39 (43, 47, 51) sts, work to end. Using separate balls of yarn and working both sides of neckline at same time, dec 1 st each neck edge every row four times, as follows:

Row 1 (WS): On right neck edge, purl to last 3 sts, p2tog-tbl, p1; on left neck edge, p1, p2tog, purl to end of row—18 (20, 22, 24) sts rem each side.

Row 2: On left edge, knit to last 3 sts, k2tog, k1; on right edge, k1, ssk, knit to end of row—17 (19, 21, 23) sts rem each side.

Rep Rows 1 and 2 once—15 (17, 19, 21) sts rem each side. Work even until piece measures same as for back. Place rem sts on holders for 3-Needle BO.

Finishing

Transfer sts from right front and back holders onto needles. With MC and 3-Needle BO (see page 156), BO all sts. Rep for left front and back sts. With MC and Mattress st (see page 156), sew side seams from armhole to waistband (do not sew waistband).

Neckband

With A and dpn, pick up and knit 72 (80, 88, 96) sts around neck opening (approximately every other st). Join sts into a circle; place marker (pm) for beg of rnd. Purl 1 rnd. BO all sts knitwise.

Armhole Edging

With A and dpn, pick up and knit 52 (55, 55, 58) sts around armhole (approximately every other st). Complete as for neckband.

Button Loops

°With A and dpn, pick up and knit 3 sts on BO edge of back of waistband, where first cable crossing occurs. Work I-Cord (see page 53) 2½" (6.5 cm) long. Cut yarn, leaving 4" (10 cm) tail. Thread needle with tail and insert through rem sts. Pull to tighten. Use tail to secure end at first cable crossing to form loop. Rep from ° at each of 3 rem cable crossings on BO edge. Sew buttons to front of waistband, opposite loops, in center of "O" of cable. Weave in all ends to WS and secure.

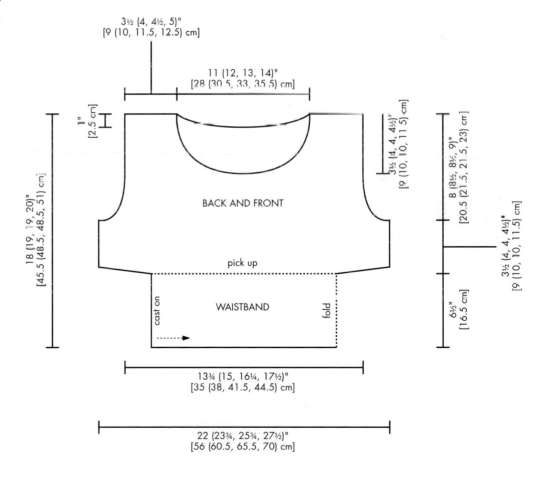

3½ (4, 4½, 5)"
[9 (10, 11.5, 12.5) cm]

11 (12, 13, 14)"
[28 (30.5, 33, 35.5) cm]

1"
[2.5 cm]

3½ (4, 4, 4½)"
[9 (10, 10, 11.5) cm]

18 (19, 19, 20)"
[45.5 (48.5, 48.5, 51) cm]

8 (8½, 8½, 9)"
[20.5 (21.5, 21.5, 23) cm]

BACK AND FRONT

pick up

3½ (4, 4, 4½)"
[9 (10, 10, 11.5) cm]

cast on

WAISTBAND

fold

6½"
[16.5 cm]

13¾ (15, 16¼, 17½)"
[35 (38, 41.5, 44.5) cm]

22 (23¾, 25¾, 27½)"
[56 (60.5, 65.5, 70) cm]

High Roller Vest

Inspired by martini glasses, this cabled vest is a sumptuous addition to your summer days. The cable pattern is a six-row repeat, making it easy to memorize. The soft cotton yarn is such pleasure to knit, you won't want to put this project down.

Finished Size

Small (Medium, Large, XLarge) 37 (41, 44, 47)" [94 (104, 112, 119.5) cm] actual chest circumference
Size shown: Small

Ingredients

525 (625, 700, 715) yds [480 (571.5, 640, 654) m] medium-weight cotton yarn in blue ⑷

Three size 5 (3.75 mm) straight knitting needles, or size to obtain gauge

Cable needle (cn)

4 stitch holders

Tapestry needle

Shown: Blue Sky Alpacas Dyed Cotton (100% organically grown cotton; 150 yds [137 m] per 100 g hank): #628 Azul, 4 (5, 5, 5) hanks

Gauge

20 sts and 28 rows = 4" (10 cm) in Stockinette stitch (St st)
Don't free pour; do a gauge swatch!

Stitch Explanation

C4B: Sl next 2 sts to cn and hold in back, k2, k2 from cn.
C4F: Sl next 2 sts to cn and hold in front, k2, k2 from cn.

Slip Stitch Rib (multiple of 3 sts):
Row 1 (RS): °P2, sl 1; rep from ° to end of row.
Row 2: °P1, k2; rep from ° to end of row.
Rep Rows 1 and 2 for pattern.

95

Tips

- Keep a nice edge for the armholes by knitting the last stitch of each row and slipping the first stitch of each row knitwise.

- Give the yarn a little tug when going from a purl to a knit stitch or from a knit to a purl stitch to avoid looseness or a slight hole. This is especially important when working the cable section.

- When adding a new hank of yarn, do it at the beginning of a row. You'll be able to weave the end into the seam for a nice professional-looking result.

Cable Pattern (panel of 16 sts; see Chart):
Setup Row 1 (RS): P6, k4, p6.
Setup Row 2: K6, p4, k6.
Setup Rows 3 and 4: Rep Setup Rows 1 and 2.
Setup Row 5: P4, C4B, C4F, p4.
Setup Row 6: K4, p8, k4.
Setup Row 7: P2, C4B, k4, C4F, p2.
Setup Row 8: K2, p12, k2.
Setup Row 9: C4B, k8, C4F.
Setup Row 10: Purl
Row 11: K4, C4B, C4F, k4.
Rows 12 and 14: Purl.
Row 13: K2, C4B, k4, C4F, k2.

Row 15: C4B, k8, C4F.
Row 16: Purl.
Rep Rows 11–16 for pattern.

Note

Slip all sts purlwise with yarn in back, unless otherwise indicated.

Back
CO 92 (104, 110, 119) sts. Knit 3 rows.

Begin Pattern
Row 1 (RS): Work in Sl St Rib to last 2 sts, p2.
Row 2: K2, work in Sl St Rib to end of row.

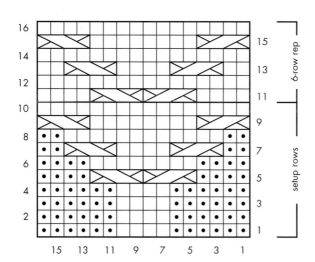

CABLE CHART

KEY

☐ Knit on RS, purl on WS.

⊡ Purl on RS, knit on WS.

⧖ C4B: Sl next 2 sts to cn and hold to back, k2, k2 from cn.

⧗ C4F: Sl next 2 sts to cn and hold to front, k2, k2 from cn.

Work even until piece measures 15 (15½, 16, 16½)" [38 (39, 40.5, 42) cm] from CO edge, ending with a WS row.

Shape Armhole (RS)
Continuing in pattern as established, binding off sts in pattern, BO 5 (6, 8, 10) sts at beg of next 2 rows, 3 (5, 5, 4) sts at beg of next 2 rows, then 3 (3, 4, 3) sts at beg of next 2 rows—70 (76, 76, 85) sts rem. Work even until piece measures 18½ (19¼, 20, 21) [47 (49, 51, 53.5) cm] from CO edge, ending with a WS row.

Shape Neck
Row 1 (RS): Work 16 (19, 19, 22) sts, p38 (38, 38, 41) sts, work to end.
Rows 2 and 3: Rep Row 1.
Row 4: Work 16 (19, 19, 22) sts, attach second ball of yarn, BO center 38 (38, 38, 41) sts, work to end of row. Using separate balls of yarn and working both sides of neckline at same time, work even for 3 (3½, 4, 4½)" [7.5 (9, 10, 11.5) cm], ending with a WS row. Place sts on holders for finishing.

Front
CO 92 (102, 110, 118) sts. Knit 3 rows.

Begin Pattern
Row 1 (RS): Work in Slip St Rib over 33 (39, 42, 45) sts, p5 (4, 5, 6), work in Cable Pattern from Chart

over 16 sts, p5 (4, 5, 6), sl 1, work in Slip St Rib to last 2 sts, p2.

Row 2: K2, work in Slip St Rib over 30 (36, 39, 42) sts, p1, k5 (4, 5, 6), work in Cable Pattern over 16 sts, p5 (4, 5, 6), work in Slip St Rib to end of row.

Work even until piece measures 15 (15½, 16, 16½)" [38 (39, 40.5, 42) cm] from CO edge, ending with a WS row.

Shape Armhole (RS)

Continuing in pattern as established, binding off sts in pattern, BO 5 (6, 8, 10) sts at beg of next 2 rows, 3 (4, 5, 4) sts at beg of next 2 rows, then 3 (4, 4, 3) sts at beg of next 2 rows—70 (74, 76, 84) sts rem. Work even until piece measures 16¾ (17½, 18¼, 19¼)" [42 (44.5, 46.5, 49) cm] from CO edge, end with Row 16 of Cable Pattern.

Shape Neck

Row 1 (RS): Work 27 (29, 30, 34) sts, k16, work to end of row.

Row 2: Work 27 (29, 30, 34) sts, p16, work to end of row.

Row 3 (RS): Work 16 (19, 19, 22) sts, p11 (10, 11, 12), p2tog, p12, p2tog, p11 (10, 11, 12), work to end of row—68 (72, 74, 82) sts rem.

Row 4: Work 16 (19, 19, 22) sts, p11 (10, 11, 12) sts, p2tog, p10, p2tog, p11 (10, 11, 12), work to end of row—66 (70, 72, 80) sts rem.

Row 5: Work 16 (19, 19, 22) sts, p11 (10, 11, 12), p2tog, p8, p2tog, p11 (10, 11, 12), work to end of row—64 (68, 70, 78) sts rem.

Row 6: Work 16 (19, 19, 22) sts, attach second ball of yarn, BO center 32 (30, 32, 34) sts purlwise. Using separate balls of yarn and working both sides of neckline at same time, work even for 4 (4½, 5, 5½)" [10 (11.5, 12.5, 14) cm], ending with a WS row. Place sts on holders for finishing.

Finishing

Transfer sts from right front and right back shoulders to separate needles. With 3-Needle BO (see page 156), BO all sts. Rep for left shoulders. Block pieces to measurements. With Mattress st (see page 156), sew side seams. Weave in all ends to WS and secure.

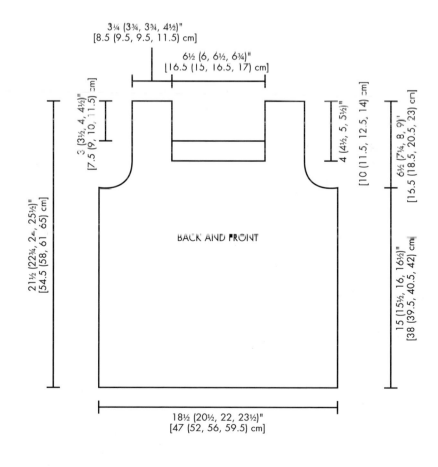

3¼ (3¾, 3¾, 4½)" [8.5 (9.5, 9.5, 11.5) cm]

6½ (6, 6½, 6¾)" [16.5 (15, 16.5, 17) cm]

3 (3½, 4, 4½)" [7.5 (9, 10, 11.5) cm]

4 (4½, 5, 5½)" [10 (11.5, 12.5, 14) cm]

6½ (7¼, 8, 9)" [16.5 (18.5, 20.5, 23) cm]

21½ (22¾, 24, 25½)" [54.5 (58, 61, 65) cm]

15 (15½, 16, 16½)" [38 (39.5, 40.5, 42) cm]

BACK AND FRONT

18½ (20½, 22, 23½)" [47 (52, 56, 59.5) cm]

Take Me Home Slippers

Lose yourself in rhythmic motion as you watch this lattice cable take shape. Inspired by a walk in a garden, the rustic charm of these slippers will comfort you on chilly evenings. An inner sole lining of "fur" provides warmth as well as cushioning. Cradled in comfort, your feet will be right at home in these dreamy slippers.

REFRESH
Knitting in the Round (page 37)

Finished Size
Small (Medium, Large)
To fit women's U.S. shoe sizes 5/6 (7/8, 9/10) [UK sizes 3 (5, 7)]
Size shown: Small (women's U.S. shoe size 5/6) [UK size 3]

Ingredients
150 yds (137 m) medium-weight wool yarn in berry (MC) 4

43 yds (39.5 m) super bulky-weight fur yarn in coordinating color (A) 6

One pair size 6 (4 mm) straight knitting needles, or size to obtain gauge

Set of five size 6 (4 mm) double-pointed knitting needles

Cable needle (cn)

Tapestry needle

Shown: Mountain Colors 4/8's Wool (100% wool; 250 yds [229 m] per 100 g hank): Berry (MC), 1 hank; Mountain Colors Wooly Feathers (65% kid mohair, 35% nylon; 85 yds [77.5 m] per 100 g hank): Raspberry (A), 1 hank

Gauge
20 sts and 28 rows = 4" (10 cm) in Stockinette stitch (St st) with MC
Don't free-pour; do a gauge swatch!

Stitch Explanation
T2F: Sl next st to cn and hold in front, p1, k1 from cn.
T2B: Sl next st to cn and hold in back, k1, p1 from cn.
C2BW: Sl next st to cn and hold in back, p1, p1 from cn.
C2FW: Sl next st to cn and hold in front, p1, p1 from cn.

Lattice Cable (multiple of 4 sts + 6):
Row 1 (RS): P1, *T2F, T2B; rep from * to last st, p1.
Row 2: K2, *C2BW, k2; rep from * to end of row.
Row 3: P1, *T2B, T2F; rep from * to last st, p1.
Row 4: K1, p1, k2, *C2FW, k2; rep from * to last 2 sts, p1, k1.
Rep Rows 1–4 for pattern.

1 × 1 Rib (multiple of 2 sts):
All Rnds: *K1, p1; rep from * to end of rnd.

Upper (make 2)

With MC and straight needles, CO 30 (38, 42) sts. Beg Lattice Cable. Work even until piece measures 4½ (5½, 6½)" [11.5 (14, 16.5) cm] from CO edge, ending with Row 3.
Dec Row (WS): [Ssk] twice, *C2FW, k2; rep from * to last 4 sts, [k2tog] twice—26 (34, 38) sts rem.
Last Row (Dec Row): *K2tog; rep from * to end of row—13 (17, 19) sts rem.
BO all sts purlwise.

Outer Sole (make 2)

Note: Slip first st of each row purlwise.
With MC and straight needles, CO 10 sts. Beg Garter St; work even for 1 row.
First Inc Row: Sl 1, kf&b, knit to last 2 sts, kf&b, k1—12 sts.
Work even until piece measures 4 (5, 6)" [10 (12.5, 15) cm] from CO edge.
Rep First Inc Row—14 sts.
Work even for 1" (2.5 cm).
Second Inc Row: Sl 1, kf&b, knit to last 2 sts, kf&b—16 sts.
Work even for ½" (1.3 cm).
Rep First Inc Row 1—18 sts.
Work even for 2½" (6.5 cm).
Dec Row: Sl 1, ssk, knit to last 3 sts, k2tog, k1—16 sts rem.
Work even for 2 rows.
BO all sts.

Inner Sole (make 2)

With A and straight needles, CO 8 sts. Beg Rev St st. Work even for 4" (10 cm), ending with a RS row.
Inc Row: K1, kf&b, knit to last 2 sts, kf&b, k1—10 sts.

Work even until piece measures 7¾ (8¾, 9¾)" [19.5 (22, 25) cm] from CO edge.
BO all sts.

Side Strip (make 2)

With MC and straight needles, CO 66 sts. Work as for upper until piece measures 2" (5 cm) from CO edge. Transfer sts to dpns. Cut yarn, leaving 1 yd (.9 m) tail.

Finishing

With MC and Mattress st (see page 156), sew narrow sides of side strip to upper as shown.

Cuff

With dpn, pick up and knit an even number of sts along rem portion of CO edge of upper, between the seams with side strip, work across side strip sts. Divide these evenly onto 4 dpn. Join A. *K2tog; rep from * to end of rnd. Beg 1 × 1 Rib. Work even for 1" (2.5 cm). BO all sts loosely in rib.

Attach Soles

With RS (purl side) of inner sole facing out, center inner sole on top of outer sole, matching toe and heel of each piece. With tapestry needle and A, sew outside edges of inner sole to ridges of outer sole, making sure that sts do not show on bottom of slipper.

Place upper/side strip piece on top of the inner sole/outer sole piece, with the WS of the upper lying on the inner sole, and the BO edge of the upper at the toe of the inner sole. With MC, sew these together as for the toes of the Long Island Iced Tea Athletic Socks (see page 29), being careful not to catch yarn from inner sole in the seam. *Note: You will be working into the side of the outer sole and the BO edge of the side strip.* Weave all ends to WS and secure.

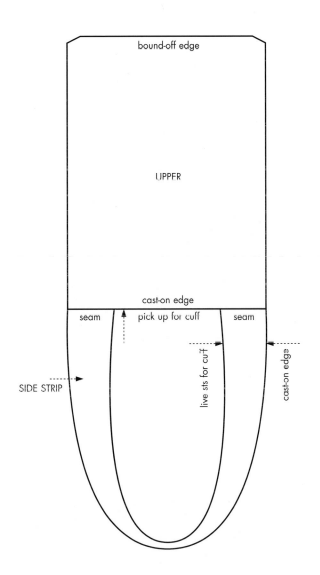

bound-off edge

UPPER

cast-on edge

seam   pick up for cuff   seam

SIDE STRIP

live sts for cuff

cast-on edge

Coffee Drinks

Feelin' Hot, Hot, Hot!

Felting is so satisfying; it reminds us of baking cookies with our grandmothers when we were little girls. Take simple, basic ingredients, put them all together, add heat, and presto! Pull out something special to enjoy yourself or to share with a friend.

What exactly is felting? Felting involves making a fabric out of compressed animal fibers. Knitters accomplish this by putting a loosely knitted fabric in a hot-water wash, usually with the aid of a washing machine and a little liquid dish soap. The resulting fabric is as tight as you want to make it, and completely unique. The fabric also hides imperfections: uneven gauge or ugly holes get closed up, so you look like a pro.

First of all, choose your yarn. Select 100 percent animal fibers, such as wool, mohair, alpaca, and llama, for best results. If you're the kind of person who likes to take risks, it is possible to felt some yarns that contain a small amount of plant or synthetic fiber. It is absolutely vital that you make a gauge swatch and run it through the felting process before you begin work on your project. No, really! Each yarn is

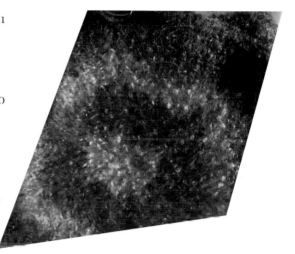

going to behave differently when you put it in the hot wash. You may find that a yarn that looks luscious in the skein loses its flavor after taking a hot bath. For example, alpaca felts to a softer fabric with more drape than wool. You might not want to use it for a purse, which needs a firm fabric to withstand everyday wear and tear. Even some 100 percent sheep's wools felt differently, depending on the breed of sheep, and superwash wool is specially treated to prevent exactly what you're trying to do. So, make sure that you don't free-pour on this one.

Knit your gauge swatch, making it 6" (15 cm) square or larger. Keep in mind that knitting to the unfelted gauge does not guarantee that the finished project will felt to the correct dimensions. Take four pieces of synthetic or plant fiber yarn and mark off a 4" (10 cm) square within the swatch (see photos, page 104). We'll use this swatch later to measure how much the square shrank after felting and compare its felted gauge with the felted gauge of the project.

Now, here comes the exciting part. Put your knitted piece in a zippered pillowcase or mesh bag (in case it sheds) and put it in the washing machine, with something heavy like a pair of old jeans for agitation. Set washer for a hot wash and put in a small amount of liquid dish soap. While it's filling up, go run and get your kitchen timer. Set the kitchen timer for 3 to 5 minutes, to remind you to stop the washer and check to see how the felting is progressing. You are in charge! When the felted piece looks like it's approaching the correct dimensions, take it out and rinse it with cold water in your sink to firm up the fabric, then gently shape to desired dimensions and place on a drying rack to dry.

When you're felting your gauge swatch, you may notice that the middle of the swatch felts faster than the outside edges. This is called splay. Don't worry, your *Yarn Cocktails* directions are written to compensate for splay. Finally, measure the 4" (10 cm) square you marked off before putting the swatch in the wash. See how much it shrank? This is your felted gauge. Shake and Bake, baby!

Unfelted swatch

Felted swatch

Vodka Espresso Felted PDA Bag

Tired of fumbling around for your PDA? This handy bag attaches to your belt loop for convenient access. Knit a rectangle lengthwise, then fold the rectangle and sew it to create the pocket and flap. Attach a swivel hook, clip the bag to your belt loop, and go. It's the perfect gift!

Finished Size

15" (38 cm) wide × 6¼" (16 cm) long, before folding and felting 4½" (11.5 cm) wide × 5¼" (13.5 cm) high (not including flap), after felting

Ingredients

48 yds (44 m) medium-weight 100% wool yarn in dark tweed (MC) **4**

46 yds (42 m) medium-weight 100% wool yarn in medium tweed (A) **4**

46 yds (42 m) medium-weight 100% wool yarn in pale tweed (B) **4**

One pair size 11 (8 mm) straight knitting needles, or size to obtain gauge

One pair size 8 (5 mm) double-pointed knitting needles (dpn)

Tapestry needle

Sew-on snap

Sewing thread to match B

Swivel hook

Shown: Cascade Yarns Eco Wool (100% natural Peruvian wool; 478 yds [437 m] per 250 g hank): #9012 dark tweed (MC), #9008 medium tweed (A), and #9004 pale tweed (B), 1 hank each

Gauge

8½ sts and 16½ rows = 4" (10 cm) in Garter St (knit every row), with larger needles and MC, before felting 8½ sts = 3" (7.5 cm); 16½ rows = 3¼" (8.5 cm) in Garter St, after felting Don't free-pour; do a gauge swatch!

Row 18 (Dec Row): Continuing in Garter St and Stripe Sequence as established, k1, *k2tog, k3; rep from * to last 3 sts, k2tog, k2—32 sts rem. Work even for 5 rows. BO all sts.

Finishing

Lay piece on flat surface with WS facing up. Fold along the long edge 6½" (16.5 cm) up, leaving 2" (5 cm) at top for flap. With MC, whip stitch sides together. Weave in all ends to WS and secure.

Felt (see page 103). Shape to measurements and lay flat to dry.

When dry, fold edge over purse pocket to form flap. With thread and tapestry needle, sew one part of snap to WS of flap, ⅜" (1 cm) below top edge of flap, and second part of snap to RS of pocket, below top edge, making sure that flap closes securely over PDA.

With MC and dpn, CO 2 sts. Work I-Cord (see page 53) for 4" (10 cm). BO all sts. Thread I-Cord through bottom loop of swivel hook, then sew ends of I-Cord to upper right-hand edge of pocket to form loop.

Stitch Explanation

Stripe Sequence: *Work 2 rows in B, 2 rows in A, then 2 rows in MC; rep from * for Stripe Sequence.

Begin Bag

With MC and larger needles, CO 32 sts. Beg Garter St (knit every row). Work even for 1 row.
Continuing in Garter St, beg Stripe Sequence.
Work even for 6 rows.
Row 8 (Inc Row): Continuing in Garter St and Stripe Sequence as established, k2, *inc 1, k4; rep from * to last 2 sts, inc 1, k2—40 sts. Work even for 9 rows.

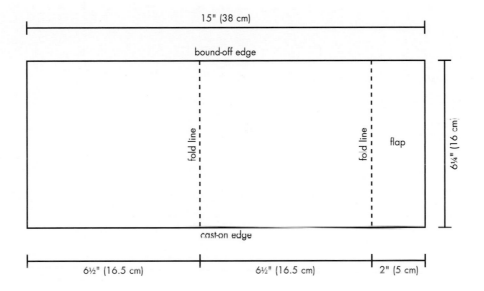

15" (38 cm)

bound-off edge

fold line

fold line

flap

6¼" (16 cm)

cast-on edge

6½" (16.5 cm) 6½" (16.5 cm) 2" (5 cm)

Café Brûlot Felted Bag

Believe it or not, this bag uses the same technique as the traditional log cabin quilt square! Add unique color placement for a more modern look. Start by knitting a small square, then turn to pick up and knit stitches on the side. No fancy, frustrating colorwork; before you know it, you're done, leaving plenty of time to relax and people-watch at your local café.

Finished Size

11½" (29 cm) wide × 10" (25.5 cm) high, after felting

Ingredients

192 yds (175.5 m) bulky-weight wool yarn in red (MC) 〔5〕

43 yds (39.5 m) bulky-weight wool yarn in orange (A) 〔5〕

9 yds (8 m) bulky-weight wool yarn in yellow (B) 〔5〕

One pair size 15 (10 mm) straight knitting needles, or size to obtain gauge

Tapestry needle

Shown: Lorna's Laces Swirl Chunky (83% merino wool, 17% silk; 120 yds [110 m] per 4 oz [114 g] hank):

#11ns Bold Red (MC), 2 hanks; #1214ns Carrot (A) and #40ns Sunshine (B), 1 hank each

Gauge

9 sts and 14 rows = 4" (10 cm) in Garter St (knit every row), before felting

10 sts and 18½ rows = 4" (10 cm) in Garter St, after felting

Don't free pour; do a gauge swatch!

Note

The entire bag is worked in Garter st. Slip the first st of each row purlwise.

108

Front and Back (make 2)

Panel 1

Using B, CO 7 sts. Beg Garter St (knit every row), slipping first st of each row. Work even for 13 rows.

Panel 2

Change to A. Work even for 13 rows. BO all sts; fasten off last st, leaving it on the needle; do not break yarn.

Panel 3

Turn work clockwise (to the right) (see Assembly Diagram, page 111). Pick up and knit 13 sts in slipped sts along left side of Panels 1 and 2—14 sts (including final st from BO of Panel 2). Work even for 13 rows. BO all sts; fasten off last st, leaving it on the needle; do not break yarn.

Panel 4

Turn work clockwise. Pick up and knit 6 sts in slipped sts along left side of Panel 3 (including final st from BO of Panel 3), and 7 sts in CO sts of Panel 1—21 sts. Work even for 13 rows. BO all sts; fasten off last st, leaving it on the needle; do not break yarn.

Panel 5

Turn work clockwise. Pick up and knit 6 sts in slipped sts along left side of Panel 4 (including final st from BO of Panel 4) and 14 sts in slipped sts along left side of Panels 1 and 2—21 sts. Work even for 13 rows.

Panel 6

Change to MC. Turn work clockwise. Pick up and knit 6 sts in slipped sts along left side of Panel 5 (including final st from BO of Panel 5), 7 sts in BO sts of Panel 2, and 7 sts in slipped sts along left side of Panel 3—21 sts. Work even for 7 rows.

Dec Row: Sl 1, (k5, k2tog) twice, k6—19 sts rem. Work even for 5 rows. BO all sts; fasten off last st, leaving it on the needle; do not break yarn.

Panel 7

Turn work clockwise. Pick up and knit 6 sts in slipped sts along left side of Panel 6 (including final st from BO of Panel 6), 14 sts in BO sts of Panel 3, and 7 sts in left side of Panel 4—28 sts. Work even for 7 rows.

Dec Row: Sl 1, (k5, k2tog) 3 times, k6—25 sts rem. Work even for 5 rows. BO all sts; fasten off last st, leaving it on the needle; do not break yarn.

Panel 8

Turn work clockwise. Pick up and knit 6 sts in slipped sts along left side of Panel 7 (including final st from BO of Panel 7), 14 sts in BO sts of Panel 4, and 7 sts in slipped sts along left side of Panel 5—28 sts. Complete as for Panel 7.

Panel 9

Turn work clockwise. Pick up and knit 6 sts in slipped sts along left side of Panel 8 (including final st from BO of Panel 8), 21 sts in BO sts of Panel 5, and 7 sts in slipped sts along left side of Panel 6—35 sts. Work even for 7 rows.

Dec Row: Sl 1, (k5, k2tog) 4 times, k6—31 sts rem. Work even for 5 rows. BO all sts.

Bottom and Side Gusset/Shoulder Strap

Using MC, CO 10 sts. Beg Garter St, slipping first st of each row. Work even until piece measures 88" (2.25 m) from CO edge (approximately 174 ridges). BO all sts.

Finishing

WS facing, beg at 36th ridge from CO edge of shoulder strap, with MC and Mattress st (see page 156), sew one side of strap along three sides of front, beg with short side first. Rep for other side of strap and back. With MC and Mattress st, sew CO and BO edges of strap together. Turn bag inside out so RS is facing. Weave in all ends to WS and secure.

Felt (see page 103). Shape to measurements and lay flat to dry.

ASSEMBLY DIAGRAM

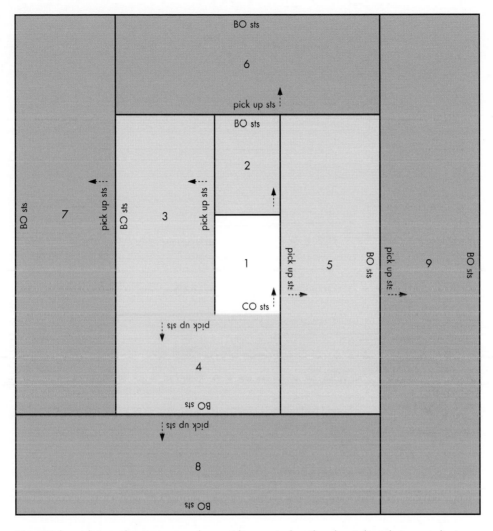

Note: Work panels in number sequence as shown, picking up sts along the edges indicated. Arrows indicate direction of work once sts are picked up.

Mexican Coffee Purse

Shaken and stirred! Hold a strand of two colors of yarn together to create your own custom color blends. We blended yellow with orange, then orange with pink, then pink with purple for a palette reminiscent of a Baja sunrise. Strategically placed decreases shape the purse and accentuate the concentric rings of color created by knitting in the round. A fabulous kid mohair/wool-blend yarn felts beautifully, for a bag that is both durable and touchable. The perfect pick-me-up!

REFRESH
Knitting in the Round
(page 37)

Finished Size

15" (38 cm) wide × 15" (38 cm) long, before felting
10" (25.5 cm) wide × 10" (25.5 cm) long, after felting

Ingredients

127 yds (116 m) fine-weight 50% kid mohair/50% wool yarn in purple (A)

160 yds (146.5 m) fine-weight 50% kid mohair/50% wool yarn in pink

92 yds (84 m) fine-weight 50% kid mohair/50% wool yarn in orange (C)

32 yds (29.5 m) fine-weight 50% kid mohair/50% wool yarn in yellow (D)

One set of five size 10½ (6.5 mm) double-pointed knitting needles (dpn), or size to obtain gauge

Stitch marker

Tapestry needle

1¼" (3 cm) square button

Sewing thread in coordinating color

Shown: Mangham Manor Yarns Shenandoah (50% kid mohair, 50% wool; 312 yds [285 m] per 177 g hank): Purple Mountain Majesty (A), Piedmont Pink (B), Markham Peach (C), and Dawn's Early Light (D), 1 hank each

Gauge

9½ sts and 15 rows = 4" (10 cm) in St st, unfelted
9½ sts = 3" (7.5 cm); 15 rows = 3.25" (8.5 cm) in Stockinette stitch, felted

Circle (make 2)

With 1 strand each of A and B held together, CO 120 sts. Divide sts between two circ needles or four dpn (optional). Join sts into a circle, being careful not to twist CO edge; place marker (pm) for beg of rnd.

Rnds 1, 3, 5, 7, 9, 11, 13, 15, 17, 19, 21, and 23: Knit.

Rnds 2, 4, and 6: Purl.

Rnd 8: *Ssk, k16, k2tog; rep from * to end of rnd—108 sts rem.

Rnd 10: Change to 1 strand each of B and C held together; drop A. *Ssk, k14, k2tog; rep from * to end of rnd—96 sts rem.

Rnd 12: Change to 1 strand each of C and D held together; drop B. *Ssk, k12, k2tog; rep from * to end of rnd—84 sts rem.

Rnd 14: *Ssk, k10, k2tog; rep from * to end of rnd—72 sts rem.

Rnd 16: Change to 1 strand each of B and C held together; drop D. *Ssk, k8, k2tog; rep from * to end of rnd—60 sts rem.

Rnd 18: *Ssk, k6, k2tog; rep from * to end of rnd—48 sts rem.

Rnd 20: *Ssk, k4, k2tog; rep from * to end of rnd—36 sts rem.

Rnd 22: Change to 1 strand each of C and D held together; drop B. *Ssk, k2, k2tog; rep from * to end of rnd—24 sts rem.

Rnd 24: *Ssk, k2tog; rep from * to end of rnd—12 sts rem.

Rnd 25: *K2tog; rep from * to end of rnd—6 sts rem.

Cut yarn, leaving a 6" (15 cm) tail. Thread tapestry needle with tail and insert through remaining sts. Pull to tighten. Weave in all ends to WS and secure.

Gusset/Shoulder Strap

With 1 strand each of A and B held together, CO 6 sts. Beg Garter St (knit every row). Work even until piece measures 54" (137 cm) from CO edge. BO all sts.

Finishing

With RS facing, using MC and Mattress st (see page 156), sew long edge of strap along CO edge of one circle, beg at 13th st of CO edge of circle, and ending at 13th st from end of CO edge of circle. Repeat with other edge of strap and second circle. With Mattress st, sew CO and BO edges of strap together.

Button Loop

With 2 dpns and 1 strand each of A and B held together, and leaving a 4" (10 cm) tail, CO 2 sts. Beg I-Cord. Work even for 2" (5 cm). BO all sts, leaving a 4" (10 cm) tail. With tails, sew button loop to top center of purse at decreases. Weave in all ends to WS and secure.

Felt (see page 103). Shape to measurements and lay flat to dry. When dry, sew button to top center of purse, opposite button loop.

Tips

- Make sure that you give a little tug to the yarn in between decreases, especially the decreases at the beg and end of the round. This will help prevent a hole that will not felt together as well as the rest of the purse.

- Seam your pieces together loosely. Tight seaming will distort the shaping of the purse after it has been felted, because the tight seams will felt at a different rate than the knit fabric.

Irish Coffee Necklace

All eyes will be smiling at you when you wear this fabulous necklace. The knitted medallions are hand-felted, so the magic of felting happens right before your eyes. Beading the medallions adds dimension and rich flavor, for a piece of jewelry that's a pleasure to create and wear.

Finished Size

18" (45.5 cm) long

Ingredients

50 yds (45.5 m) lightweight mohair/wool/nylon-blend yarn in autumn colors ▣③

One pair size 4 (3.5 mm) straight knitting needles

40 g (size 11/0) seed beads in green frost (A)

40 g (size 11/0) seed beads in blue/green frost (B)

4 Austrian crystal cubes in burgundy (C)

Size 10 beading needle

Flexible twisted beading needle

Size 0 nylon beading thread in tan

1 yd (.9 m) clear nylon beading cord (transite)

2 gold knot covers

2 clear seed beads

Hook-and-eye clasp in gold

Small bowl

Measuring teaspoon

Tapestry needle

Jeweler's glue

Needle-nose or chain-nose pliers

Shown: Plymouth Yarn Company, Inc. Adriafil Collection Bacio (73% mohair, 22% wool, 5% nylon; 50 g per ball): #40, 1 ball; Fire Mountain Gems Dyna-Mites 11/0 seed beads in Frost AB Jade Green (A) and Frost AB Peacock Green (B); Austrian Crystal Burgundy Cubes (C); vermeil hook-and-eye clasp; Nymo beading thread

Gauge

Not essential for necklace

Medallion (make 9)
CO 3 sts.
Row 1 (RS): [Kf&b, k1] in each st—9 sts.
Row 2 and all WS rows: Purl.
Row 3: *Kf&b; rep from * to end of row—18 sts.
Row 5: Knit.
Row 7: *K2tog; rep from * to end of row—9 sts rem.
Row 9: *Sk2p; rep from * to end of row—3 sts rem.
Cut yarn, leaving a 6" (15 cm) tail. Thread tapestry needle with tail and insert through rem sts. Pull to tighten. Fold piece in half so CO and BO ends are together. Whip stitch side seams to form circle. Weave in all ends to WS and secure.

115

Hand Felting

Prepare a tub of hot water (as hot as you can stand it) and a tub of ice water. Apply liquid dish soap to one medallion and briskly rub the fabric in the hot water. Increase the agitation by using a stiff-bristled brush like a kitchen or nail brush, or even rub two medallions together. Continue to rub the circles, alternating between the hot and cold water baths. When the fabric has felted sufficiently, rinse well. Squeeze out excess water with a towel. Form into a medallion shape and allow to dry completely on a screen mesh or wire rack for air flow.

Beading Side Medallions (make 8)

Scoop 3 teaspoons each of A and B seed beads into small bowl and stir. Cut a 24" (61 cm) length of beading thread. Knot one end and thread the other end through size 10 beading needle.

Step 1:
Anchor thread into medallion fabric by inserting needle through edge of circle.

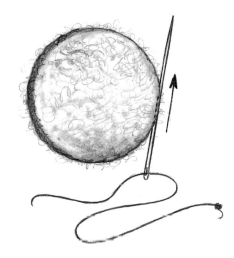

Step 2:
Pull thread through and insert again at point where thread exited the medallion. This will lock the thread in place. Now you're ready to bead.

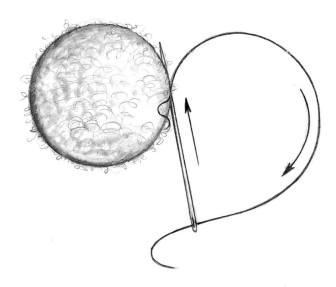

Work Backstitch Technique around edge of circle: *Slide 6 seed beads onto thread, then press them down onto fabric. Insert needle into fabric where last bead lies and bring needle back up between third and fourth beads. Insert needle back through last 3 beads. Rep from * around edge of medallion. Turn medallion over and bead other side in same manner. There should be a space of approximately ¼" (6 mm) between the 2 beaded edgings around the circumference of the circle. Using A only, work a smaller circle in the same manner, just inside the top edging. This will be the RS of the medallion.

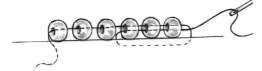

Fasten off by weaving thread through fabric and tying surgeon's knot by first tying an overhand knot, wrapping right end of cord around left end several times.

Then, tie a regular overhand knot with left cord over right. Rep for 7 more medallions.

Beading Center Medallion

Bead center medallion as above, but in reverse, using only A in the outer circle, and an A and B mixture in the inner circle. After completing circles, bring needle through side of medallion, between outer edgings. Slide 6 B, 1 C, then 3 B seed beads onto thread. Insert needle back through next-to-last bead, then all other beads, and back into medallion. Fasten off by weaving thread through medallion and tying surgeon's knot, as shown.

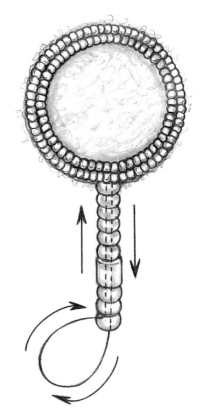

Stringing the Necklace

Tie a surgeon's knot approximately 3" (7.5 cm) from end of clear nylon cord; pull tightly. With flexible beading needle, slide on one clear seed bead, and insert needle through bead again as shown.

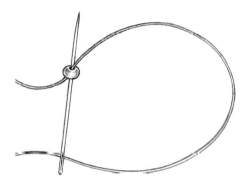

This will lock the bead in place when you slide it to the knot. Slide on one knot cover as shown.

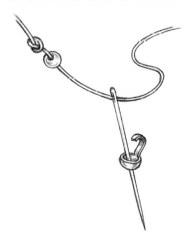

Trim clear nylon cord inside knot cover and place jeweler's glue on cut end to prevent knot from coming out. Do not close knot cover.

Slide on 33 B beads. *Insert needle through end of one side of medallion, between beaded edgings, approximately ⅛" (3 mm) from edge and slide onto beading cord. Slide on 18 B beads. Rep from * once.

Sliding remaining medallions as for first, string the rest of the necklace as follows:

One side medallion, 6 B beads, 1 C bead, 6 B beads; one side medallion, 15 B beads; center medallion, 15 B beads; one side medallion, 6 B beads, 1 C bead, 6 B beads; **one side medallion, then 18 B beads. Rep from ** once. Slide on final side medallion, then 33 B beads.

Slide on another knot cover through bottom of cover (as opposed to through top as for first knot cover).

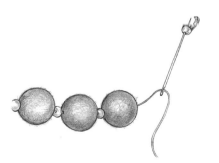

Slide on a clear seed bead and insert needle through the bead again. Move seed bead and knot cover next to last bead. Knot clear nylon cord.

Trim cord and apply jeweler's glue to cut end. Close knot covers around jump rings on clasp, using needle-nose or chain-nose pliers.

Garnish with a Twist

On the Cutting Edge

From lacy and elegant to fresh and fun, edgings are more than just a finishing touch; they are your personal signature on your garment. The choices are limitless when it comes to trimming your knitting. We will show you our favorites: ruffles, lace, and fringe. You may knit your edging directly onto the garment as you go, or you may knit your edging separately and add it on later. There are advantages to both methods. Adding the edging to the garment as you knit it saves time and makes it easy to correctly measure the edging. See our Blue Knickers design (page 122) for a picot waistband that is knitted into the garment. If you work the edging separately, you'll be able to sew the trimming to an existing piece or apply an edging to a garment in a way that doesn't follow the stitch direction (ie. adding an edging at a diagonal when the piece is worked horizontally). Make sure the edging piece is the correct length. See the Tantalize Cocktail Skirt (see page 127) for this type of edging. The bottom of the skirt is worked separately and from side to side, then sewn to the body of the skirt.

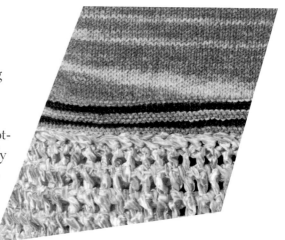

Edgings don't even have to be added to the "edge" of your piece. They can be applied to the center of the fabric (as in the cord for Blue Knickers), or connected around to add stability to a piece (see the cord in Tropical Dream Camisole [see page 81]), or worked by themselves (Frozen Fruit Daiquiri Necklace [see page 62]).

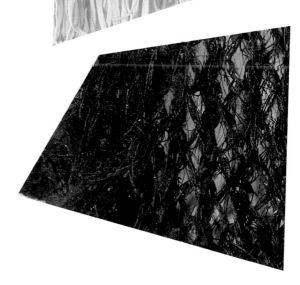

Blue Knickers

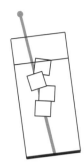

Put your best side forward with these undies. Worked in two pieces, they provide coverage without sacrificing style. An unobtrusive edging adds flavor, and there's a little surprise on the back: an I-Cord heart! Work them in a corn yarn that is hydroscopic and comfortable. Bottoms up!

REFRESH
I-Cord (page 53)

Finished Size
XSmall (Small, Medium, Large, XLarge)
26 (30, 34, 38, 42)" [66 (76, 86.5, 96.5, 106.5) cm] actual waist circumference
Size shown: XSmall

Ingredients
200 (375, 460, 550, 645) yds [183 (343, 420.5, 503, 590) m] medium-weight yarn in blue (MC) **4**

56 (66, 76, 96, 116) yds [51 (60.5, 69.5, 88, 106) m] medium-weight yarn in variegated blue/white (A) **4**

5 yds (4.5 m) medium-weight yarn in pink (B) **4**

One pair size 6 (4 mm) straight knitting needles, or size to obtain gauge

One pair size 3 (3.25 mm) double-pointed knitting needles (dpn)

Stitch holder

1 (1, 1½, 1½, 1½) yd [.9 (.9, 1.4, 1.4, 1.4) m] ¼" (6 mm) -wide elastic

Sewing needle and thread

Tapestry needle

Shown: South West Trading Company aMAIZing (100% corn fiber; 142 yds [130 m] per 50 g ball): #159 Little Boy Blue (MC), 2 (3, 4, 4, 5) balls; #162 Aidan (A) and #157 Princess (B), 1 ball each

Gauge
20 sts and 28 rows = 4" (10 cm) in Stockinette stitch (St st), with larger needles
Don't free-pour; do a gauge swatch!

Stitch Explanation
P2tog-tbl: Purl 2 stitches together through the back loops.

Back
With MC and larger needles, CO 65 (75, 85, 95, 105) sts.
Rows 1, 3, 5, 9, 11, and 13 (RS): Knit.
Row 2 and all WS rows: Purl.
Row 7 (Picot Turning Row): K1, *yo, k2tog; rep from * to end of row.
Row 14: Purl.

Back side of Blue Knickers

Work even in St st for 6 (6, 8, 10, 12) rows.

Inc Row 1 (RS): Inc 1 st each side this row, every eight rows 0 (2, 3, 4, 4) times, then every six rows 4 (2, 1, 0, 0) times, as follows: K2, inc 1-R, knit to last 2 sts, inc 1-L, k2—75 (85, 95, 105, 115) sts. Purl 1 row. Work even for 6 rows.

Shape Legs

(RS) Continuing in St st, BO 5 (9, 9, 12, 12) sts at beg of next 2 rows—65 (67, 77, 81, 91) sts rem.

Rows 1 and 3: K1, [ssk] 1 (1, 1, 1, 2) times, knit to last 3 (3, 3, 3, 5) sts, [k2tog] 1 (1, 1, 1, 2) times, k1—59 (61, 71, 75, 81) sts rem after row 3.

Rows 2, 4, 6, 8, 10, 12, 14, 16, and 18: P1, p2tog, purl to last 3 sts, p2tog-tbl, p1—15 (15, 15, 15, 17) sts rem after row 18.

Row 5: K1, [ssk] 1 (1, 2, 2, 3) times, knit to last 3 (3, 5, 5, 7) sts, [k2tog] 1 (1, 2, 2, 3) times, k1—55 (57, 65, 69, 73) sts rem.

Row 7: K1, [ssk] 2 (2, 2, 3, 3) times, knit to last 5 (5, 5, 7, 7) sts, [k2tog] 2 (2, 2, 3, 3) times, k1—49 (51, 59, 61, 65) sts rem.

Row 9: K1, [ssk] 2 (2, 3, 4, 4) times, knit to last 5 (5, 7, 9, 9) sts, [k2tog] 2 (2, 3, 4, 4) times, k1—43 (45, 51, 51, 55) sts rem.

Front side of Blue Knickers

Row 11: K1, [ssk] 3 (3, 4, 4, 4) times, knit to last 7 (7, 9, 9, 9) sts, [k2tog] 3 (3, 4, 4, 4) times—35 (37, 41, 41, 45) sts rem.

Row 13: K1, [ssk] 2 (3, 4, 4, 4) times, knit to last 5 (7, 9, 9, 9) sts, [k2tog] 2 (3, 4, 4, 4) times—29 (29, 31, 31, 35) sts rem.

Row 15: K1, [ssk] 2 (2, 3, 3, 3) times, knit to last 5 (5, 7, 7, 9) sts, [k2tog] 2 (2, 3, 3, 3) times—23 (23, 23, 23, 27) sts rem.

Row 17: K1, [ssk] 2 (2, 2, 2, 3) times, knit to last 5 (5, 5, 5, 7) sts, [k2tog] 2 (2, 2, 2, 3) times—17 (17, 17, 17, 19) sts rem.

Row 19: Rep Row 1—13 sts rem. Continuing in St st, starting with WS row, work even for 7 rows. Place sts on holder for finishing.

Front

Work as for back through Row 14. Work even in St st for 14 (14, 14, 16, 16) rows.

Inc Row 1 (RS): Inc 1 st each side this row, every twelve rows 0 (0, 0, 1, 2) times, every ten rows 0 (1, 2, 1, 0) times, then every eight rows 2 (1, 0, 0, 0) times, as follows: K2, inc 1-R, knit to last 2 sts, inc 1-L, k2—71 (81, 91, 101, 111) sts. Work even for 7 (9, 11, 11, 11) rows.

Shape Legs

(RS) Continuing in St st, BO 10 (12, 14, 16, 18) sts at beg of next two rows, 5 (6, 7, 8, 9) sts at beg of next six rows, then dec 1 st each side every other row four times, as follows: K1, ssk, work to last 3 sts, k2tog, k1, ending with a WS row—13 sts rem. Work even for 11 rows.

Finishing

Transfer sts from back holder to needle. With 3-Needle BO (see page 156), BO rem sts from front and back.

Heart

With B and dpn, CO 3 sts. Beg I Cord. Work even until piece measures 6½" (16.5 cm). BO all sts. Sew CO and BO edges together. Pin I-Cord to back in the form of a heart (see photo on page 123). Sew in place.

Picot Edging

With RS of front facing, beg at right front side edge, at beg of leg shaping, with A and larger needles, pick up and knit 1 st in each st along leg opening, ending at right back side edge. Make sure you have an even number of sts. Purl 1 row.

Picot Row (RS): BO 2 sts, *sl rem st from right-hand needle back to left-hand needle, with Cable CO (see page 149), CO 3 sts, BO 5 sts;

rep from * to end of row. Fasten off. Rep for left leg opening.

Waistband

With Mattress st (see page 156), sew side seams. Measure waist. Cut piece of elastic 2" (5 cm) shorter than waist measurement. Overlap ends of elastic and sew together. Fold waistband over elastic to WS at picot turning row and sew to WS, being careful not to catch elastic or let sts show on RS. Weave in all ends to WS and secure.

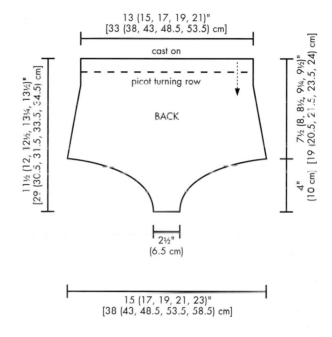

13 (15, 17, 19, 21)"
[33 (38, 43, 48.5, 53.5) cm]

cast on

picot turning row

BACK

11½ (12, 12½, 13¼, 13½)"
[29 (30.5, 31.5, 33.5, 34.5) cm]

7½ (8, 8½, 9¼, 9½)"
[19 (20.5, 21.5, 23.5, 24) cm]

4"
(10 cm)

2½"
(6.5 cm)

15 (17, 19, 21, 23)"
[38 (43, 48.5, 53.5, 58.5) cm]

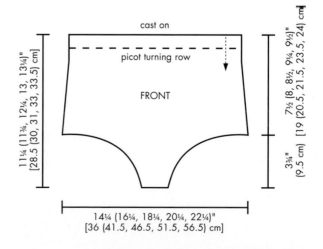

cast on

picot turning row

FRONT

11¼ (11¾, 12¼, 13, 13¼)"
[28.5 (30, 31, 33, 33.5) cm]

7½ (8, 8½, 9¼, 9½)"
[19 (20.5, 21.5, 23.5, 24) cm]

3¾"
(9.5 cm)

14¼ (16¼, 18¼, 20¼, 22¼)"
[36 (41.5, 46.5, 51.5, 56.5) cm]

Tantalize Cocktail Skirt

Inspired by warm tropical sunsets, this skirt is perfect for strolling along the beach. Changing colors is a breeze; just wrap the new color around the right needle and complete a stitch as usual. Knit the lace edging and attach it after the body of the skirt is complete. It's a romantic ending to this tantalizing design.

REFRESH
Knitting in the Round
(page 37)

Finished Size

Small (Medium, Large, XLarge)
32 (36¼, 40¾, 45)" [81.5 (92, 103.5, 114.5) cm] waist circumference, 20½ (21½, 22½, 23½)" [52 (54.5, 57, 59.5) cm] long
Size shown: Medium

Ingredients

680 (800, 910, 1050) yds [622 (731.5, 832, 960) m] lightweight wool/nylon-blend yarn in peach (MC) (**3**)

40 (45, 50, 55) yds [36.5 (41, 45.5, 50.5) m] lightweight silk yarn in brown (A) (**3**)

95 (105, 115, 125) yds [87 (96, 105, 114.5) m] bulky-weight ribbon yarn in peach (B) (**5**)

One size 3 (3.25 mm) 32" (81.5 cm) -long circular (circ) knitting needle, or size to obtain gauge

One pair size 13 (9 mm) straight knitting needles

5 stitch markers, including 1 in contrasting color

Tapestry needle

Shown: Fiesta Yarns Socorro (82% wool, 18% nylon; 210 yds [192 m] per 4 oz [114 g] hank): #27144 Pink Champagne (MC), 4 (4, 5, 6) hanks; Fiesta Yarns La Luz (100% spun silk; 210 yds [192 m] per 2 oz [57 g] hank): #3327 Vanilla Bean (A), 1 hank; Fiesta Yarns Verandah (90% nylon, 7% rayon, 3% polyester; 130 yds [119 m] per 4 oz [114 g] hank): #26145 White Zinfandel (B), 1 hank

Gauge

22 sts and 32 rows = 4" (10 cm) in Stockinette stitch (St st) with MC and circ needle
Don't free-pour; do a gauge swatch!

127

Stitch Explanation

Yo twice: Wrap yarn around knitting needle as for a regular yo, then wrap yarn around needle again before working next st. This is a 2-stitch increase.

Knit into front and back of double yo: Knit into the front loop and slip off of needle. Then knit into the back loop, which is the second yo, and complete st.

Lace Border (multiple of 2 sts + 1):

Rows 1, 3, 5, and 7 (RS): Knit.
Rows 2 and 6: K2, *yo, k2tog; rep from * to last st, yo, k1—14 sts after row 6.
Rows 4 and 8: K2, *yo, k2tog; rep from * to last 2 sts, yo, k2—15 sts after row 8.
Row 9: BO 4 sts, knit to end of row—11 sts rem.
Rep Rows 2–9 for pattern.

Waistband

With circ needle and MC, CO 176 (200, 224, 248) sts. Join sts into a circle, being careful not to twist CO edge; place contrasting color marker (pm) for beg of rnd.

Rnds 1, 5, and 8: Purl.
Rnds 2 and 3: Change to A; knit.
Rnd 4: Change to MC; knit.
Rnd 6 (Eyelet Rnd): *K2tog, yo twice, k2tog; rep from * to end of rnd—176 (200, 224, 248) sts.
Rnd 7: *K1, knit into front and back of double yo, k1; rep from * to end of rnd—176 (200, 224, 248) sts.
Rnds 9–12: Change to A; knit.
Rnds 13–15: Change to MC; purl.

Body of Skirt

Knit 3 (3, 3, 4) rnds.
Inc Setup Rnd: K16, pm, inc 1-R, k56 (68, 80, 92), pm, inc 1-R, k32, pm, inc 1-R, k56 (68, 80, 92), pm, inc 1-R, k16—180 (204, 228, 252) sts. Knit 3 (3, 3, 4) rnds.
Inc Rnd: Inc 4 sts this rnd, every 4 (4, 4, 5) rnds 8 (4, 0, 10) times, then every 5 (5, 5, 6) rnds 4 (8, 12, 2) times, as follows: Knit to first marker, sl marker (sm), [inc 1-R, knit to next marker, sm] 3 times, inc 1-R, knit to end of rnd—232 (256, 280, 304) sts.
Work even until piece measures 16 (17, 18, 19)" [40.5 (43, 45.5, 48.5) cm] from CO edge. *Note: Adjust length here as desired by working more or fewer rnds.*

Bottom Band

Rnds 1, 6, 7, and 12: Purl.
Rnds 2–4 and 8–10: Change to A; knit.
Rnds 5 and 11: Change to MC; knit.
Rnds 13 and 14: Knit.
BO all sts loosely.

Lace Border

With larger needles and B, CO 11 sts. Beg Lace Border pattern. Work even until piece measures 42¼ (46½, 51, 55¼)" [107.5 (118, 129.5, 140.5) cm] from CO edge, ending with Row 9 of pattern. BO all sts.

Finishing

With MC, beg at center back of bottom band of skirt, sew straight edge of lace border to bottom band. Sew CO and BO edges of lace border together. Weave in all ends to WS and secure.

Drawstring

Cut one strand of B 62 (66, 70, 74)" [157.5 (167.5, 178, 188) cm] long, or to desired length. Weave drawstring through eyelets in waistband.

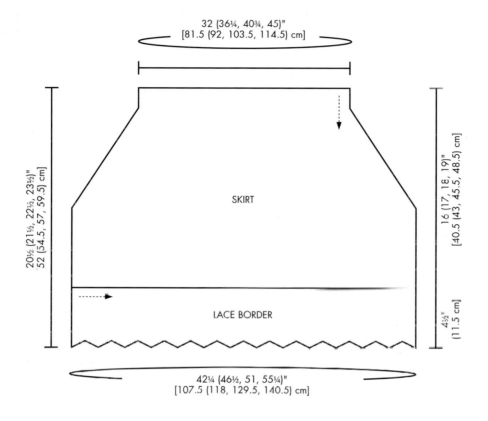

32 (36¼, 40¾, 45)"
[81.5 (92, 103.5, 114.5) cm]

SKIRT

LACE BORDER

20½ (21½, 22½, 23½)"
52 (54.5, 57, 59.5) cm]

16 (17, 18, 19)"
[40.5 (43, 45.5, 48.5) cm]

4½"
(11.5 cm)

42¼ (46½, 51, 55¼)"
[107.5 (118, 129.5, 140.5) cm]

Day Dream Fringed Corset

Hey, cowgirls! Lasso that cute cowboy, when you wear this seductive corset. The front points and stitch pattern details add a slimming effect. Pick up your needles and knit a romantic corset with Wild West flair.

Finished Size

Small (Medium, Large, XLarge)
30 (34, 38, 42)" [76 (86.5, 96.5, 106.5) cm] actual chest circumference
Size shown: Small

Ingredients

470 (555, 640, 735) yds [430 (507.5, 585, 672) m] medium-weight nylon yarn in blue (MC) (**4**)

30 (40, 50, 60) yds [27.5 (36.5, 45.5, 55) m] medium-weight nylon yarn in ivory (CC) (**4**)

One pair size 7 (4.5 mm) straight knitting needles, or size to obtain gauge

Size F/5 (3.75 mm) crochet hook

2 yds (1.8 m) fine hemp twine

4 stitch holders

Tapestry needle

Shown: Berroco Suede (100% nylon; 120 yds [110 m] per 50 g ball): #3789 Nelly Belle (MC), 4 (5, 6, 7) balls; #3727 Dale Evans (CC), 1 ball

Gauge

20 sts and 28 rows = 4" (10 cm) in Stockinette St (St st)
Don't free-pour; do a gauge swatch!

Stitch Explanation

Purled CO: With WS facing and yarn in front, *purl first st on left-hand needle, then instead of sliding st from needle, sl loop just made onto left-hand needle. Rep from * for number of sts required.

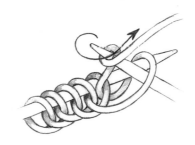

Note

The left and right front points are worked first, then sts are cast on for the sides and back, and the body is worked back and forth in one piece.

Left Front Point

With MC, CO 1 st.
Row 1 (RS): Kf&b—2 sts.
Row 2: P1, inc 1, p1—3 sts.
Row 3: Kf&b, knit to end of row—4 sts.
Row 4: Purl to last st, inc 1, p1—5 sts.
Rows 5–18: Rep Rows 3 and 4—19 sts after row 18.
Row 19: Rep Row 3—20 sts. Transfer sts to stitch holder.

Right Front Point

With MC, CO 1 st.
Row 1 (RS): Kf&b—2 sts.
Row 2: P1, inc 1, p1—3 sts.
Row 3 (RS): Knit to last st, kf&b—4 sts.

131

Row 4: P1, inc 1, purl to end of row—5 sts.

Rows 5–18: Rep Rows 3 and 4—19 sts after Row 18.

Row 19: Rep Row 3—20 sts. Turn work, ready to work body.

Body

WS facing, with Purled CO, CO 110 (130, 150, 170) sts, turn work so RS is facing, knit across 20 sts from holder for left front point—150 (170, 190, 210) sts.
(WS) Beg St st. Work even for 15 rows.

For Size Medium Only

Work even for 2 rows.

For Size Large Only

Work even for 6 rows.

For Size XLarge Only

Work even for 10 rows.

Begin Vertical Pattern

Rows 1, 3, 5, and 7 (RS): K10, p1, k2, p1, knit to last 14 sts, p1, k2, p1, knit to end of row.

Row 2 and all WS rows: Purl.

Rows 9, 11, 13, and 15: K10, *p1, k2, p1, k4, p1, k2, p1*, knit to last 22 sts; rep from * to *, knit to end of row.

Rows 17, 19, 21, 23, 25, 27, and

29: K10, *(p1, k2, p1, k4) twice, p1, k2, p1*, knit to last 30 sts; rep from * to *, knit to end of row.

Rows 31, 33, 35, and 37: K18, *p1, k2, p1, k4, p1, k2, p1*, knit to last 30 sts; rep from * to *, knit to end of row.

Rows 39, 41, 43, and 45: K26, p1, k2, p1, knit to last 30 sts, p1, k2, p1, knit to end of row.

Rows 47, 49, 51, 53, 55, 57, 59–62, and 64–66: Knit.

Row 63 (Eyelet Row): K2, *k2tog, yo; rep from * to last 2 sts, k2.

Row 67: BO 19 (22, 24, 29) sts, k4, place last 5 sts worked (including st from BO) on holder for right front shoulder strap, k1, BO 28 (30, 36, 36) sts, k4, place last 5 sts worked on second holder for right back shoulder strap, k1, BO 36 (46, 50, 60) sts, k4, place last 5 sts worked on third holder for left back shoulder strap, k1, BO 28 (30, 36, 36) sts, k4, place last 5 sts worked on fourth holder for left front shoulder strap, k1, BO 19 (22, 24, 29) sts.

Shoulder Straps

WS facing, rejoin MC to sts from holder for right front shoulder strap. Knit 1 row.

Beg Garter St, slipping the first st of each row purlwise. Work even until piece measures 6 (6½, 7, 7½)" [15 (16.5, 18, 19) cm]. Transfer sts to holder for finishing. *Note: Because the straps are worked in Garter Stitch, they will stretch approximately 2" (5 cm) for a total armhole measurement of 8 (8½, 9, 9½)" [20.5 (21.5, 23, 24) cm].*

Rep for right back shoulder strap. Using 3-Needle BO (see page 156), BO right shoulder straps. Rep for left shoulder straps.

Fringe

Cut 6" (15 cm) lengths of CC. Holding two lengths together, fold them in half. Use crochet hook to pull the fold through st at bottom edge of corset. Pull cut ends through loop. Apply fringe along sts at bottom edge of corset. Trim with scissors for even lengths.

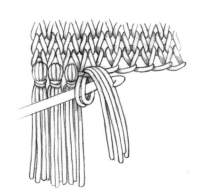

Finishing

Lay piece RS down on flat surface. Fold outside edges in so they meet in the center. Lace hemp, beg on WS, through third st from center edge, 2½" (6.5 cm) from bottom point. Lace as you would a shoe, crossing from side to side every ¾" (2 cm) up front of piece, making sure to keep ends of hemp at equal lengths. Tie bow at top. Knot ends of hemp and allow to fray. Weave in all yarn ends to WS and secure.

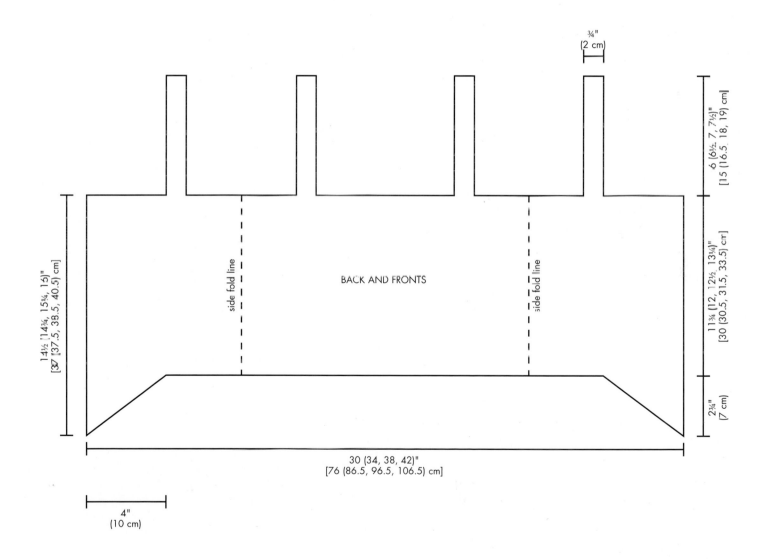

¾"
(2 cm)

6 (6½, 7, 7½)"
[15 (16.5, 18, 19) cm]

side fold line

side fold line

BACK AND FRONTS

14½ (14¾, 15¼, 16)"
[37 (37.5, 38.5, 40.5) cm]

11¾ (12, 12½, 13¼)"
[30 (30.5, 31.5, 33.5) cm]

2¾"
(7 cm)

30 (34, 38, 42)"
[76 (86.5, 96.5, 106.5) cm]

4"
(10 cm)

Fizzing Cherry Lace Vest with Ruffles

Oh, this is decadent! Treat yourself to this gorgeous, effervescent lace vest garnished with a ruffle. Use an easy lace pattern on big needles for the body of the vest, then pick up stitches around the edge with a circular needle to work your ruffle in the round. A delicious multistrand yarn makes a fabric that dips and swirls around your body. The perfect accent to a special evening, this vest is absolutely the cherry on top!

REFRESH
Knitting in the Round
(page 37)

Finished Size

Small (Medium, Large) to fit 32 34 (36–38, 40–42)" [81.5–86.5 (91.5–96.5, 101.5–106.5) cm] bust 34¼ (36½, 38¾)" [87 (92.5, 98.5) cm] actual chest circumference
Size shown: Small

Ingredients

90 (100, 110) yds [82 (91.5, 100.5) m] medium-weight mohair/viscose/polyamide/polyester multistrand yarn in burgundy (MC) (**4**)

275 (310, 345) yds [251.5 (283.5, 315.5) m] medium-weight mohair/viscose/polyamide multistrand yarn in burgundy (A) (**4**)

One pair size 15 (10 mm) knitting needles, or size to obtain gauge

One size 9 (5.5 mm) 32" (81.5 cm) -long circular (circ) knitting needle

One size 9 (5.5 mm) 16" (40.5 cm) -long circular (circ) knitting needle

Stitch marker

Crochet hook (optional)

Tapestry needle

Shown: Kolláge Yarns Splendor (mohair/viscose/polyamide/polyester; 100 yds [91.5 m] per 85 g hank): Merlot (MC), 1 (1, 2) hanks; Kolláge Yarns Inspiration (mohair/viscose; 100 yds [91.5 m] per 60 g hank): Gemstone (A), 3 (4, 4) hanks

Gauge

7 sts and 8 rows = 4" (10 cm) in Openwork Pattern with larger needles and MC

Note

Use Openwork Pattern below for gauge swatch only.
Don't free-pour; do a gauge swatch!

Stitch Explanation

Openwork Pattern (for gauge swatch only)
(multiple of 2 sts):
All Rows: K2, *yo, k2tog; rep from * to last 2 sts, k2.

Body

Note: Vest is worked back and forth in one piece to the armholes, then fronts and back are worked separately.
With larger needles and MC, CO 8 sts. Knit 1 row.
Row 1: K2, *yo, k2tog; rep from * to last 2 sts, k2.

Tips

- Use wooden needles for this project if possible, so the lace doesn't slide all over the place.

- If you are even a little familiar with using a crochet hook, it is much easier to begin the ruffle border by single crocheting the number of required stitches into the edge, then picking up and knitting into the single crochet. You can pick up all those stitches without worrying about them falling off your circular needle, and the single crochet provides a stable edge for the ruffle to originate from.

- You may use double-pointed needles to work the armhole edging, if you wish.

Row 5: BO 1 st, k1 (0, 1), [yo, k2tog] 3 (4, 4) times, k2—10 (11, 12) sts rem.

Row 6: BO 1 st, [yo, k2tog] 3 (4, 4) times, k2 (1, 2)—9 (10, 11) sts rem.

Row 7: BO 1 st, k0 (1, 0), [yo, k2tog] 3 (3, 4) times, k1 (1, 1)—8 (9, 10) sts rem.

Row 8: K1 (1, 1), [yo, k2tog] 3 (3, 4) times, k1 (2, 1).

Row 9: K1 (2, 1), [yo, k2tog] 3 (3, 4) times, k1 (1, 1).

Rows 10 and 11: Rep Rows 8 and 9.

Shape Neck

Row 12: BO 1 st, k1 (1, 1), [yo, k2tog] 2 (2, 3) times, k1 (2, 1)—7 (8, 9) sts rem.

Row 13: K1 (2, 1), [yo, k2tog] 2 (2, 3) times, k2.

Row 14: BO 1 st, [yo, k2tog] 2 (2, 3) times, k1 (2, 1)—6 (7, 8) sts rem.

Row 15: K1 (2, 1), [yo, k2tog] 2 (2, 3) times, k1.

For Sizes Medium and Large Only

Row 16: BO 1 st, k0 (1), [yo, k2tog] twice, k1—6 (7) sts rem.

Row 17: K1, [yo, k2tog] twice, k1 (2).

Row 2 (Inc Row): With Cable CO (see page 149), CO 4 sts, k2, yo, k2tog across these 4 sts, *yo, k2tog; rep from * to end of row—12 sts. Rep Row 2 every row 12 (13, 14) times—60 (64, 68) sts. Rep Row 1 every row 8 (10, 12) times.

Divide for Fronts and Back (RS): K2, [yo, k2tog] 6 (7, 7) times, k2 (1, 2); place next 28 (30, 32) sts on holder for back, then next 16 (17, 18) sts on second holder for left front.

Right Front

Shape Armhole and Neck

Row 1: BO 2 sts for armhole, k1 (0, 1), [yo, k2tog] 5 (6, 6) times, k2—14 (15, 16) sts rem.

Row 2: BO 1 st, [yo, k2tog] 5 (6, 6) times, k2 (1, 2)—13 (14, 16) sts rem.

Row 3: BO 1 st, k0 (1, 0), [yo, k2tog] 5 (5, 6) times, k1 (1, 1)—12 (13, 14) sts rem.

Row 4: BO 1 st, k1 (1,1), [yo, k2tog] 4 (4, 5) times, k1 (2, 1)—11 (12, 13) sts rem.

For Size Large Only

Row 18: BO 1 st, [yo, k2tog] twice, k1—6 sts rem.

Row 19: K1, [yo, k2tog] twice, k1.

For All Sizes

Rep Row 15 (17, 19) three times. BO all sts knitwise.

Back

Transfer 28 (30, 32) sts from back holder to needle. RS facing, attach MC at right armhole edge.

Shape Armholes

Row 1: BO 2 sts for armhole, k2, [yo, k2tog] 11 (12, 13) times, k2—26 (28, 30) sts rem.

Row 2: BO 2 sts for armhole, k2, [yo, k2tog] 10 (11, 12) times, k2—24 (26, 28) sts rem.

Row 3: BO 1 st, [yo, k2tog] 10 (11, 12) times, k2—23 (25, 27) sts rem.

Row 4: BO 1 st, [yo, k2tog] 10 (11, 12) times, k1—22 (24, 26) sts rem.

Row 5: BO 1 st, k1, [yo, k2tog] 9 (10, 11) times, k1—21 (23, 25) sts rem.

Row 6: BO 1 st, k1, [yo, k2tog] 8 (9, 10) times, k2—20 (22, 24) sts rem.

Row 7: BO 1 st, [yo, k2tog] 8 (9, 10) times, k2—19 (21, 23) sts rem.

Row 8: BO 1 st, [yo, k2tog] 8 (9, 10) times, k1—18 (20, 22) sts rem.

Row 9: K1, [yo, k2tog] 8 (9, 10) times, k1.

Rep Row 9 nine (eleven, thirteen) times.

BO all sts knitwise.

Left Front

Transfer 16 (17, 18) sts from left front holder to needle. RS facing, attach MC at armhole edge. Complete as for right front.

Attach Back to Fronts

Sew shoulder seams.

Ruffle Border

With A and longer circ needle, beg at back neck, pick up and knit 175 (190, 205) sts around entire vest. Join sts into a circle; place marker (pm) for beg of rnd.

Rnds 1, 3, and 5–8: Knit.

Rnds 2 and 4: *K1, inc 1; rep from * to end of rnd—700 (760, 820) sts after rnd 4.

Rnd 9: Purl.

Rnd 10: Knit. BO all sts knitwise.

Armhole Edging

With A and shorter circ needle, pick up and knit 60 (70, 80) sts around armhole opening. Join sts into a circle; pm for beg of rnd.

Rnd 1: Purl.

Rnd 2: Knit. BO all sts knitwise. Weave in all ends to WS and secure.

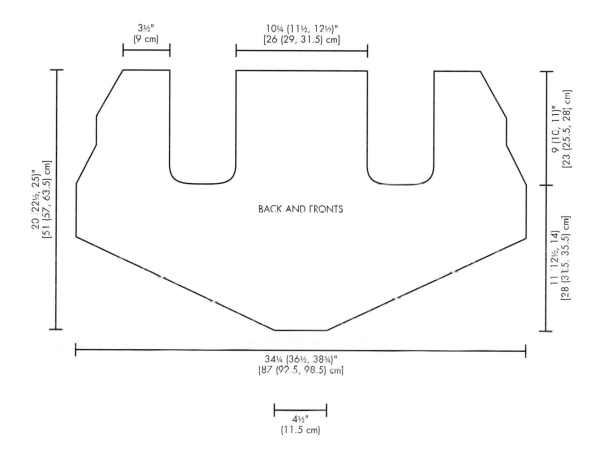

3½"
(9 cm)

10¼ (11½, 12⅓)"
[26 (29, 31.5) cm]

9 (10, 11)"
[23 (25.5, 28] cm]

20 (22½, 25)"
[51 (57, 63.5) cm]

BACK AND FRONTS

11 (12½, 14)"
[28 (31.5, 35.5) cm]

34¼ (36½, 38¾)"
[87 (92.5, 98.5) cm]

4½"
(11.5 cm)

139

Cheers!

Throw Your Own Yarn Cocktails *Party!*

Statistically, we spend more and more time working and commuting, leaving less time for relaxation and socializing. Knitting is by nature a community activity, so gather your friends together for a fun and relaxing evening of knitting by hosting your own *Yarn Cocktails* party.

The key ingredients to a *Yarn Cocktails* party are good food, good friends, and good yarn. After that, the theme can be extended as far as you wish.

When preparing a menu for a *Yarn Cocktails* party, select foods that will not prevent your guests from enjoying their knitting. Finger foods such as fresh fruit or cheese served with toothpicks will allow your guests to stab their food and keep their hands clean. For fun, put toothpicks in bite-size meatballs to represent balls of yarn with needles. It doesn't hurt to have moist towelettes on hand, just in case. A skein of licorice laces tangled together with some knitting needles makes a conversation piece that your guests will enjoy unraveling or perhaps even knitting. You may choose to extend the *Yarn Cocktails* theme to include drinks. Recipes for the

drinks that inspired the patterns in this book are included on page 143. A word of warning: As the host, you are responsible for the safety of your guests. Think yarn over, not hangover! Encourage your guests to drink responsibly, and if guests do imbibe, do not let them drive. Your intervention could save a life.

Present your guests with a smorgasbord of yarns. Arrange a variety of small balls of coordinating yarns in large cocktail glasses. Invite each guest to select a ball from each glass and a pair of knitting needles and swatch away. Each swatch is sewn together into a scarf. Hold a drawing for the finished scarf, which the winner can keep and wear as a memento of the party.

For a fun game, gather around and hold your own fastest-knitter competition. You can make a game into a great charity activity by choosing an easy hat or scarf pattern. Challenge your guests to knit as many as they can during the party, then donate the finished items to a charity.

Everyone loves a goody bag. Stuff it with inexpensive, useful favors such as row counters, stitch markers, coilless safety pins, and needle gauges.

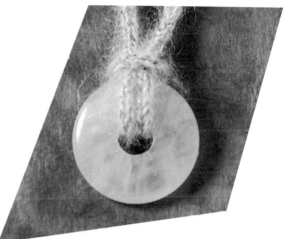

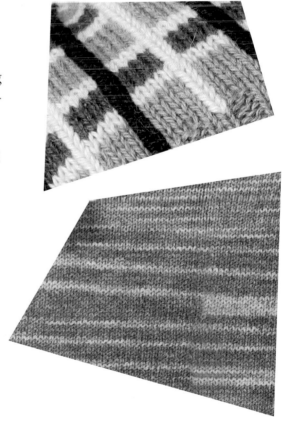

For a great icebreaker, make your own sparkling row counters! You'll need:

24" (61 cm) length of nylon beading cord (or transite used in our jewelry designs)

10 (6 mm) Swarovski Pearls in Peach

2 (4 mm) Swarovski Round Faceted Crystals in clear AB

1 (4 mm) Swarovski Round Faceted Crystal in peach

Hoop earring wire or split ring marker

Jeweler's glue

Step 1

Fold the beading cord in half. Slide on the hoop earring wire or split ring marker and position it in the center of fold.

Step 2

Slide on a bead, crossing the left and right ends of the cord. The right end will go through the bead hole from right to left. The left end will go through the hole from left to right. Holding the beading cord down on a table with a heavy object helps when doing this step.

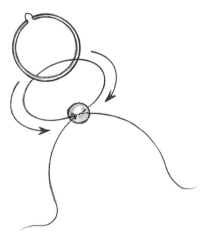

Step 3

Insert cords through several more beads in the same manner. Adjust each bead so that it will be centered before adding another bead.

Rep Step 3 until all beads have been attached. Holding both ends of cord together, tie knot 1 to 1½" (2.5 to 4 cm) from the last bead. Slide the 4 mm beads onto cords held together. Tie another knot to secure. Apply a drop of jeweler's glue to the knot. The 6 mm beads slide up and down, allowing you to keep track of your rows or repeats.

Recipes

Here are some cocktail recipes, so go stir up some fun!

CHAPTER 1
Classic Cocktails

Singapore Sling

1½ ounces (42 ml) gin

½ ounce (14 ml) cherry liqueur

¼ ounce (7 ml) orange liqueur

¼ ounce (7 ml) brandy liqueur

4 ounces (120 ml) pineapple juice

½ ounce (14 ml) lime juice

⅓ ounce (10 ml) grenadine

1 dash bitters

1 maraschino cherry, for garnish

1 slice pineapple, for garnish

Shake all the liquid ingredients with ice. Strain into an ice-filled Collins glass. Garnish with a cherry and a slice of pineapple.

Deep Blue Sea

1½ ounces (42 ml) peach schnapps

1½ ounces (42 ml) Blue Curaçao

1½ ounces (42 ml) bitter lemon

1½ ounces (42 ml) lime cordial

1 slice lemon, for garnish

Build the liquid ingredients over ice cubes. Garnish with a lemon slice.

Long Island Iced Tea

1 part vodka

1 part tequila

1 part rum

1 part gin

1 part Triple Sec

1½ parts sweet-and-sour mix

1 splash cola

1 slice lemon, for garnish

Mix the liquid ingredients together over ice in a glass. Pour into a shaker and give one brisk shake. Pour back into the glass and make sure there is a touch of fizz at the top. Garnish with a lemon slice.

Tequila Sunrise

2 ounces (60 ml) tequila

orange juice

2 dashes grenadine syrup

Pour the tequila in a highball glass with ice, and fill to the top with orange juice. Stir. Add the grenadine syrup, flipping the bottle vertically very quickly while tilting the glass and pouring the syrup down the side. The grenadine should go straight to the bottom and then rise slowly up through the drink.

CHAPTER 2
Frozen Drinks

Watermelon Daiquiri

2½ cups (585 ml) seedless water-melon, cut into 1" (2.5 cm) cubes

1 tablespoon (15 ml) freshly squeezed lime juice

4 ounces (120 ml) tequila

2 ounces (60 ml) orange-flavored liqueur

1½ cups (355 ml) crushed ice

1 lime wheel or watermelon wedge, for garnish

Put the cut watermelon in a plastic bag and freeze for a minimum of 2 hours. If time does not permit freezing, add a few extra ice cubes when blending. Stuff all the ingredients into a blender and purée until smooth. Garnish the rim of a glass with a lime wheel or watermelon wedge. Serve immediately.

Snow Blinder

2 ounces (60 ml) vodka

2 scoops vanilla ice cream

8 ounces (235 ml) lemonade

Pour the vodka into a blender and add the ice cream. Blend. Top with lemonade.

Banana Boat

2 ounces (60 ml) melon-flavored liqueur

1 ounce (28 ml) banana-flavored liqueur

1 ounce (28 ml) Blue Curaçao

8–10 ounces (236–285 ml) pine-apple juice

1 long banana, peeled

1 slice pineapple, for garnish

Place the banana into a medium-size glass and add cracked ice. Combine in another glass all other ingredients except the pineapple, and pour over the ice. Add the pineapple slice and enjoy.

Blackberry Smoothie

2 ounces (60 ml) blackberry brandy

2 cups (280 g) vanilla ice cream

Combine the vanilla ice cream and brandy in a blender. Blend until smooth, pour into a hurricane glass, and serve.

CHAPTER 3
Champagne Drinks

Blue Fizz

½ ounce (14 ml) Blue Curaçao

2 ounces (60 ml) gin

½ ounce (14 ml) lemon juice

2 ounces (60 ml) sugar

3 ounces (90 ml) club soda

Measure a Collins glass full of ice cubes into a cocktail shaker. Add all ingredients except the club soda. Shake and pour back into the glass. Add the club soda and stir.

Flirtini

2 pieces fresh pineapple

½ ounce (14 ml) orange-flavored liqueur

½ ounce (14 ml) vodka

1 ounce (28 ml) pineapple juice

3 ounces (90 ml) champagne

1 maraschino cherry, for garnish

Muddle the pineapple pieces and orange-flavored liqueur in the bottom of a mixing glass. Add the vodka and pineapple juice, and stir. Strain into a chilled cocktail glass and top with champagne. Garnish with a cherry.

Frozen Fruit Daiquiri

1¼ ounces (35 ml) white rum

2–3 dashes dark rum

2–3 dashes syrup

½ teaspoon (1 g) powdered sugar

Fruit pieces

¾ ounce (21 ml) lime juice

Blend all ingredients with crushed ice in a blender. Pour into a cocktail glass and serve.

Disco Fizz

¾ ounce (21 ml) Blue Curaçao

champagne

1½ ounces (42 ml) pineapple juice

1 dash lemon juice

¾ ounce (21 ml) elderflower cordial

1 twist of lemon, for garnish

Pour all liquid ingredients into a champagne flute and top up with champagne. Garnish with a lemon twist.

CHAPTER 4
Tropical Drinks

Cuba Libre

2 ounces (60 ml) light rum

Juice of ½ lime

6 ounces (175 ml) cola

Pour the lime juice into a highball glass over ice cubes. Add the rum, fill with cola, stir, and serve.

Blue Bayou

1 cup (235 ml) ice

1½ (12 ml) ounces vodka

½ ounce (14 ml) Blue Curaçao

½ cup (77 g) fresh pineapple

2 ounces (60 ml) grapefruit juice

1 chunk pineapple, for garnish

Pour all ingredients except garnish into a blender and blend until smooth. Then pour into a margarita glass and top with a chunk of pineapple.

Honey Rum Swizzle

1½ ounces (42 ml) dark rum

3 dashes bitters

¾ ounce (21 ml) lime juice

1½ teaspoons (8 ml) honey

1 teaspoon (4 g) sugar

1 lime wheel, for garnish

Half fill a glass with crushed ice. Shake the liquid ingredients, honey, and sugar together in a cocktail shaker with ice, and strain into the glass. Mix in the glass with a muddling spoon until the glass frosts. Garnish with a lime wheel.

Tropical Dream

1 part coconut rum

1 part Blue Curaçao

1 part pineapple juice

1 maraschino cherry, for garnish

Shake the three liquid ingredients together and pour in to a cocktail glass. Garnish with a cherry on the rim of the glass.

CHAPTER 5
Martini Drinks

Dry Martini

2 parts dry gin

1 part French vermouth

1 dash bitters

1 twist of lemon, for garnish

1 green olive, for garnish

Mix the gin, vermouth, and bitters. Serve with a twist of lemon on top and a green olive skewered on a wooden pick.

After Dark Martini

3 ounces (90 ml) vodka

1½ ounces (42 ml) white crème de cacao

¾ ounce (21 ml) green crème de menthe

¾ ounce (21 ml) dry vermouth

Stir all ingredients with ice and strain into a glass.

High Roller

1½ (42 ml) ounces gin

¾ ounce (21 ml) triple sec

¾ ounce (21 ml) apricot brandy

1½ ounces (42 ml) dry vermouth

1 physalis fruit, for garnish (optional)

Mix the ingredients together in a cocktail shaker with ice. Strain into a cocktail glass. Add a physalis fruit if desired, as garnish.

Take Me Home

2 parts Scotch-blend whiskey

1 part white crème de cacao

1 part aniseed-flavored liqueur

Stir with ice and strain into a cocktail glass.

CHAPTER 6
Coffee Drinks

Vodka Espresso

1½ (42 ml) ounces vodka

3 ounces (90 ml) espresso coffee

2 teaspoons (8 g) sugar

1 shot Amarula Cream liqueur

Shake vodka, coffee, and sugar together with cubed ice. Strain into a glass and layer with Amarula Cream liqueur on top.

Café Brûlot

Peel of 1 orange, cut into small strips

Peel of 1 lemon, cut into small strips

4 sugar cubes

6 whole cloves

1 (2" [5 cm]) cinnamon stick

½ cup (118 ml) orange-flavored liqueur

2 cups (473 ml) hot, freshly brewed, strong black coffee

Peel of 1 orange, cut into one long, intact spiral

Light the burner under a brûlot bowl or chafing dish, and adjust the flame to low. Place the orange and lemon strips, sugar, cloves, cinnamon stick, and orange liqueur into the bowl. Cook for 1 to 2 minutes, stirring constantly with a long-handled heatproof ladle, to dissolve the sugar and warm ingredients. When warm, stir in the hot coffee, and ignite with a match. Quickly, while the mixture is still flaming, hold the spiraled orange peel with the prongs of a fork over the bowl, and ladle the flaming coffee mixture down the peel several times into the bowl for a spectacular presentation. Ladle into demitasse cups, being careful to leave peels, cinnamon stick, and cloves in the bowl. Serve immediately while hot.

Mexican Coffee

5 ounces (150 ml) black coffee

1 ounce (28 ml) coffee-flavored liqueur

1 teaspoon (4 g) sugar

1½ ounces (42 ml) whipped cream

Shaved chocolate, for garnish (optional)

Pour coffee and coffee liqueur into a coffee cup. Sweeten with the sugar. Gently place the whipped cream on top and garnish with shaved chocolate if desired.

Irish Coffee

1½ ounces (42 ml) Irish whiskey

1 teaspoon (4 g) brown sugar

6 ounces (175 ml) hot coffee

Heavy cream, chilled

Combine the whiskey, sugar, and coffee in a mug and stir to dissolve. Float the cream gently on top. Do not mix.

Garnish With a Twist

Blue Knickers

1½ ounces (42 ml) vodka

1½ ounces (42 ml) Blue Curaçao

1½ ounces (42 ml) Italian herbal liqueur

pineapple juice

1 dash cream

1 orange wedge, for garnish

Shake the vodka, Curaçao, Italian herbal liqueur, and pineapple juice in a shaker. Pour into a glass and add a layer of cream on the top. Serve with a straw and an orange wedge. Drink is to be sipped through a straw.

Tantalize Cocktail

2 dashes bitters

1½ ounces (42 ml) apricot brandy

¾ ounce (21 ml) pineapple juice

¾ ounce (21 ml) lemon juice

ginger ale

1 drop grenadine

Shake all ingredients except ginger ale and grenadine with ice, then pour into a glass. Fill to the top with ginger ale and finally add a drop of grenadine to float on top of the cocktail.

Day Dream

¾ ounce (21 ml) gin

⅓ ounce (10 ml) Blue Curaçao

¾ ounce (21 ml) dry vermouth

1½ ounces (42 ml) champagne

⅓ ounce (10 ml) white grape juice

1 slice kiwi, for garnish

Mix all liquid ingredients together in a cocktail shaker and pour into a flute glass. Garnish with a slice of kiwi.

Fizzing Cherry

1½ shots cherry brandy

3 ounces (90 ml) orange juice

1½ ounces (42 ml) lime juice

¾ ounce (21 ml) sugar syrup

lemonade

1 orange or lime wedge, for garnish

Shake the first four ingredients and strain into a glass half filled with cubed ice. Fill to the top with lemonade and gently stir. Garnish with a wedge of orange or lime.

147

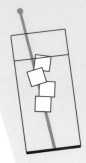

Maybe You Need a Refresher Course

Slip Knot

Step 1

Before casting on, make a slip knot. Loop yarn around in a circle and let tail hang in back. Pull the tail slightly through the circle with a knitting needle.

Step 2

With the new loop on your needle, pull the working yarn and tail to tighten.

Cast On (CO)

There are over fifty different ways to cast on. Here are the ones we like.

Long-Tail Cast-On

Step 1

After placing a slip knot on needle, place tail over left thumb, and working yarn over index finger. Hold both yarns with last three fingers on left hand. Pick up the closest loop at the thumb with point of the needle.

Step 2

Bring the point of the needle around the working yarn at index finger.

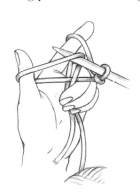

Step 3

Continue moving the point of the needle down through the loop at thumb.

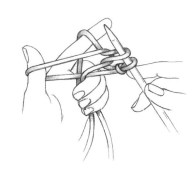

Step 4

Tighten the loop before casting on the next stitch.

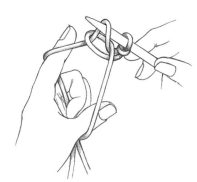

Cable Cast-On

We use this cast-on when we already have stitches on our needle and are going to cast on at the beginning of a row. Insert right-hand needle between the last two stitches on the left-hand needle. Wrap yarn around the right-hand needle counterclockwise, as you normally would when knitting a stitch, and pull up a loop. Slip this loop onto the left-hand needle.

Backward Loop Cast-On

Step 1

Begin with a slip knot on needle. Twist yarn around thumb.

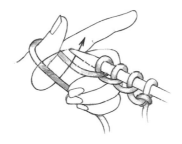

Step 2

Insert needle into twisted loop.

Step 3

Pull to tighten loop.

Knit (k)

Step 1

With yarn in back, insert point of right-hand needle into first stitch on left-hand needle (tip of needle will point away from you).

Step 2

Wrap yarn around right-hand needle counterclockwise. Pull the wrap forward through the stitch, keeping the wrap on the right-hand needle.

Step 3

Slip stitch off left-hand needle. The knit stitch is complete.

149

Purl (p)

Step 1

With yarn in front, insert point of right-hand needle into first stitch on left-hand needle (tip of needle will point toward you).

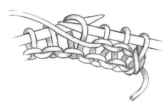

Step 2

Wrap yarn around right-hand needle counterclockwise. Push the wrap back through the stitch, keeping the wrap on the right-hand needle.

Step 3

Slip stitch off left-hand needle. The purl stitch is complete.

Garter Stitch

Knit every stitch on every row to achieve a cushiony, stretchy fabric with lots of ridges. The fabric looks the same on both sides.

Knitting every stitch

This look may also be achieved by purling every stitch on every row (see swatch below). One ridge is equal to two knitted (or purled) rows. Garter stitch doesn't roll, so it's good for the edges of sweaters and blankets.

Purling every stitch

Stockinette Stitch

Knit every stitch in one row then purl every stitch in the next row. Alternate these two rows to create a flatter fabric than Garter stitch. This fabric will have V's on the right side and ridges on the wrong side. Stockinette stitch fabric curls at the top and bottom, and the sides roll in.

Right side of Stockinette stitch

Wrong side of Stockinette stitch

Short Rows

Believe it or not, you don't actually have to work all the way to the end of the row. You can work part of a row, turn your work and begin the next row, leaving the stitches that you don't need inactive on the needles. This is known as the short-row technique, because you are making the rows shorter without increasing or decreasing stitches on the ends of the fabric. Piece of cake, right? There's a catch, though. Just turning the work will leave a hole, so you must wrap the stitch before you turn the work.

Here's how to wrap for short rows:

Step 1

Work in pattern to the stitch where you want to turn your work. Bring your yarn to the front of the work as if to purl (it may already be there if you just worked a purl stitch). Slip the stitch to be wrapped to the right-hand needle.

Step 2

Bring your yarn to the back of the work, around the front of the stitch, then slip the stitch back to the left-hand needle.

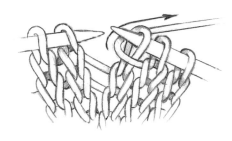

Step 3

Turn your work, ready to begin the next row (you may have to bring the yarn to the back of the work if the next stitch to be worked is a knit stitch). Continue in pattern over only the desired section.

Step 4

When it's time to reactivate the reserved stitches and start knitting them again, insert the right-hand needle into both the wrap and the stitch and knit them together (or purl them together if working purl stitches).

Short rows do not increase or decrease the number of overall stitches, so when you have finished your short rows, you should still have the same number of stitches you did originally.

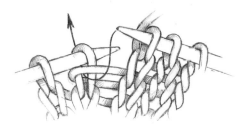

Working knit stitches

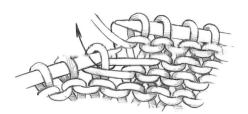

Working purl stitches

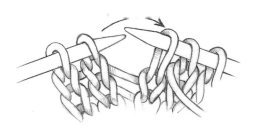

151

Slip Stitches

Slip as if to Knit

Insert the right-hand needle into the stitch from front to back as for knitting, but do not wrap the yarn around the needle. Instead, just slip the stitch off the left-hand needle. This is usually worked with the yarn in back, but the pattern may call for you to slip the stitch with the yarn in front. The term for that would be "slip 1 wyif."

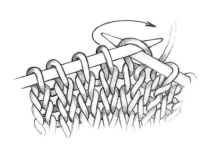

Slip as if to Purl

Insert the right-hand needle into the stitch from back to front as for purling, but do not wrap the yarn around the needle. Instead, just slip the stitch off of the left-hand needle. This is usually worked with the yarn in back, but the pattern may call for you to slip the stitch with the yarn in front. The term for that would be "slip 1 wyif."

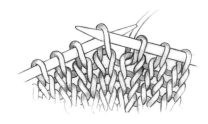

Increases (inc)

There are lots of ways to increase or add stitches to your knitting. Patterns may specify a type of increase, or just indicate to increase. In that instance, choose the increase that you like best. Here are the ones we like best.

Knit into Front and Back of a Loop (kf&b)
Step 1

Insert the needle into the front loop of the stitch, wrap the yarn around the needle and pull up a loop as for a knit stitch. Do not slip it off the left-hand needle.

Step 2

Insert the needle into the back loop of the same stitch, wrap the yarn around the needle and pull up a loop. Now slip the stitch off the left-hand needle. There should be 2 sts created from one on your right-hand needle.

Make One (inc 1)

This is an easy increase that works well in the middle of a row or round. On a knit row with the yarn in back, twist a loop of yarn around your thumb or finger and place it on the right-hand needle. This is called an inc 1-L and it slants to the left. If you twist the loop in the opposite direction, it will slant to the right and is abbreviated inc 1-R.

Notice that by twisting the loops in opposite directions before slipping them onto the needle, the two increases in the illustration are symmetrical.

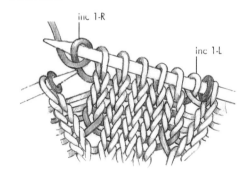

If this increase is to be worked on a purl row, with yarn in front, twist the loop of yarn around your thumb or finger and place it on the right-hand needle. This is an inc 1-P. On the next row, knit into the back of the increase loop.

Yarn Over (yo)

When making a yo between 2 knit stitches, bring the yarn forward between the needles, as for purling. Then, knit into the next st on the left-hand needle. The yo shows as a diagonal wrap around the right-hand needle and is an increase. Yarnovers create holes, so they are wonderful for lace.

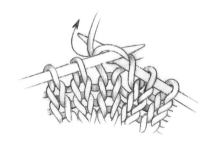

Decreases (dec)

Just like increases, there are also many decreases. Some decreases lean to the right, some to the left. If symmetry is important, the pattern will specify the decrease to use. Here are some of our favorites.

Knit Two Together (k2tog)

With yarn in back, insert the right-hand needle into the next two sts on the left-hand needle, from left to right. Knit them together. Two stitches have been decreased to one stitch.

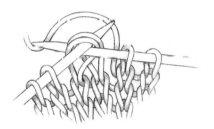

Purl Two Together (p2tog)

With yarn in front, insert the right-hand needle into the next two sts on the left-hand needle, from right to left. Purl them together. Two stitches have been decreased to one stitch.

Slip, Slip, Knit (ssk)

Slip a stitch to the right-hand needle as if to knit. Slip another stitch as if to knit. Insert the tip of the left-hand needle into these two sts, from left to right, and knit them together.

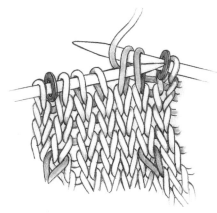

Double Centered Decrease (dcd)

Step 1

Insert the needle into the first two stitches on the left-hand needle as if you were going to work a k2tog and slip them onto the right-hand needle.

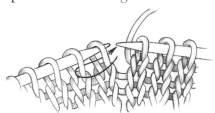

Step 2

Knit the next stitch on the left-hand needle.

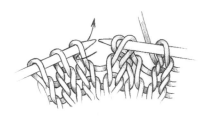

Step 3

Pass the two slipped stitches over the one just knitted.

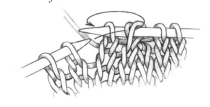

Step 4

The center stitch will be on top. Three stitches have been decreased to one.

Triple Centered Decrease (tcd)

Step 1

Slip two stitches to the right-hand needle as if you were going to work a k2tog (see Step 1 for the Double Centered Decrease).

Step 2

Knit two stitches together as for a k2tog.

Step 3

Pass the two slipped stitches over the ones just knitted. Four stitches have been decreased to one.

Picking Up Stitches

Create new stitches by knitting into the edge of a piece of knitting. This is also called "pick up and knit."

Step 1

With right side facing, insert a knitting needle into a stitch at the edge of fabric. Go through the entire stitch to the back of the fabric, not just one strand of it. Wrap the yarn around the needle and pull a loop through the fabric.

Step 2

Keep the picked-up stitches on the knitting needle.

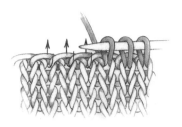

Picking Up Stitches around a Curve

You need to pick up more stitches when adding stitches along a curve versus a straight edge, as illustrated by the arrows.

Changing Colors

When it is time to change colors, loop your new color around the right-hand needle as you normally would to complete a stitch. Leave at least a 6" (15 cm) tail; you'll weave this in later. This method also works for adding a new ball of yarn. When working with two colors on the same row or round, bring the new color under the old one and complete the stitch as usual. Do not pull the yarns too tightly as this will cause puckering. When changing colors while working back and forth in rows, try to change colors or yarns at the beginning or end of the row. It will make weaving in your ends easier and less noticeable. Of course, this is not possible when knitting in the round.

Binding Off

There are over twenty-five different ways to bind off. We'll show you the basic technique.

Basic Bind-Off in Knitting

Knit two stitches. Use the point of the left-hand needle to lift the bottom stitch on the right-hand needle up and over the top stitch and off the needle. This is counted as one bind-off stitch. Knit another stitch and pass the bottom one up and off the needle. This is one more bind-off stitch. You don't count the number of stitches you have knitted, but instead, you count the number of times you have passed the bottom stitch over the top and off the needle.

When binding off purlwise, purl two stitches. Use the point of the left-hand needle to pull the bottom stitch over the top stitch and off the tip of the right-hand needle. Moving the working yarn to the back before binding off may make it easier to grab the bottom stitch; just remember to move the yarn to the front again before purling the next stitch.

When binding off in pattern, work the stitches in the set pattern one at a time. After you work a stitch, pass the bottom stitch up and off the tip of the right-hand needle.

155

3-Needle Bind-Off

With the same number of stitches on each needle, place them parallel to each other with right sides facing each other. Working on the wrong side, insert a third needle into the first stitch on each needle. Knit them together. Then, knit the next stitches together in the same manner. As for the Basic Bind-Off, lift the bottom stitch up and off the tip of the right-hand needle. This bind-off is great for shoulder seams.

Fastening Off

After binding off or finishing a piece, the yarn is cut, leaving at least a 6" (15 cm) tail, which is then pulled through the final loop. This tail will be woven into the fabric when finishing the project.

Mattress Stitch

This method creates an invisible seam. Match up the edges of fabric to be sewn together. The right side of both pieces should be facing you. Use a tapestry needle to go under the bar between the last two stitches on the left fabric. Then, go under the bar between the last two stitches at the edge of the right fabric. Pull the yarn just enough so that the edges of the fabrics come together, but not so tightly that they pucker. Alternate between the left and right fabrics as you continue sewing.

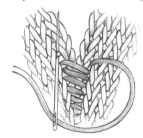

Whip Stitch

Match up the edges of fabric to be sewn together with their right sides facing each other. Insert the tapestry needle in the edge of each row, joining the two pieces.

Weave in Ends

Always leave at least a 6" (15 cm) tail for weaving. Working the ends back into the fabric secures them, and the fabric remains stretchy. Weave in enough of the tails into the wrong side of the fabric so that if they come out, there will be enough yarn to weave them back in.

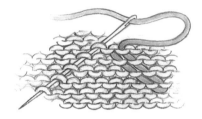

Tips

- We strongly recommend that you do not tie knots unless specified in a pattern. Instead, leave long tails when adding a new yarn and weave in your ends. This way, there won't be any knots poking up and ruining the look of your piece.

- When a loose, stretchy bind-off is desired, try binding off the stitches with a larger-size knitting needle.

Resources

Thirsty for more? Check out *Yarn Cocktails* purse-size patterns at your local yarn shop. To find a shop near you, hop over to www.anastasiaknits.com.

Check out these fantastic companies who produce luscious yarns, beads, and other great products. They graciously provided products for this book:

Alpaca with a Twist
4272 Evans Jacobi Road
Georgetown, IN 47122-9708 USA
(866) 378 9478
www.alpacawithatwist.com

Artistic Visions Design
9400 Woodcrest Road
Pittsburgh, PA 15237 USA
(412) 512-3100
www.artisticvisionsdesign.com
Handcrafted glass closures

Berroco
P.O. Box 367
Uxbridge, MA 01569 USA
(508) 278-2527
www.berroco.com

Blue Heron Yarns
29532 Canvasback Drive
Suite #6
Easton, MD 21601 USA
(410) 819-0401
www.blueheronyarns.com

Blue Sky Alpacas
P.O. Box 88
Cedar, MN 55011 USA
www.blueskyalpacas.com

Cascade Yarns
1224 Andover Park E
Tukwila, WA 98188-3905 USA
(206) 574-0440
www.cascadeyarns.com

Fiesta Yarns
5401 San Diego NE
Albuquerque, NM 87113 2901 USA
(505) 892-5008
www.fiestayarns.com

Fire Mountain Gems and Beads
One Fire Mountain Way
Grants Pass, OR 97526 USA
(800) 355-2137
www.firemountaingems.com

Hamilton Fhiber and Glass
www.hamfhiberandglass.com

Kolláge Yarns
3304 Blue Bell Lane
Birmingham, AL 35242 USA
(205) 908-1570
www.kollageyarns.com

Kraemer Yarns
P.O. Box 72
240 S Main Street
Nazareth, PA 18064-0072 USA
(610) 759-4030
www.kraemeryarns.com

Lorna's Laces
(773) 935-3803
www.lornaslaces.net

Louet North America
808 Commerce Park Drive
Ogdensburg, NY 13669 USA
(613) 925-4502
www.louet.com

Mangham Manor Wool and Mohair Farm
901 Hammocks Gap Road
Charlottesville, VA 22911 USA
(434) 973-2222
www.wool.us
Custom-dyed yarns

Mountain Colors
P.O. Box 156
Corvallis, MT 59828 USA
(406) 961-1900
www.mountaincolors.com

Muench Yarns Inc.
1323 Scott Street
Petaluma, CA 94954 USA
(707) 763-9377
www.muenchyarns.com
www.myyarns.com

Plymouth Yarn Co., Inc.
P.O. Box 28
Bristol, PA 19007 USA
(215) 788-0459
www.plymouthyarn.com

Prym Consumer USA
P.O. Box 5028
Spartanburg, SC 29304 USA
www.dritz.com

Sewing Expressions, LLC
1497 Main Street
Suite 315
Dunedin, FL 34698 USA
(727) 734-1123
www.sewingexpressions.com
Hand moisturizer

South West Trading Company
918 South Park Lane
Suite 102
Tempe, AZ 85281 USA
(480) 894-1818
www.soysilk.com

Swarovski North America Limited
One Kenney Drive
Cranston, RI 02920 USA
(401) 447-7314
www.swarovski.com
www.create-your-style.com

Tahki Stacy Charles, Inc.
70-30 80th Street, Bldg. 36
Ridgewood, NY 11385 USA
(800) 338-YARN
www.tahkistacycharles.com

Tilli Tomas, Inc.
Boston, MA USA
(617) 524-3330
www.tillitomas.com

About the Authors

Anastasia Blaes and Kelly Wilson are revitalizing knitting and crochet techniques with their focus on innovative constructions. Not afraid to push the envelope, they apply traditional techniques in a nontraditional manner to create garments and accessories that ignite the passions of knitters and crocheters, beginner and experienced alike. Anastasia owns Anastasiaknits, home of Yarn Cocktails purse-size patterns; Kelly owns Kelly Wilson Designs.

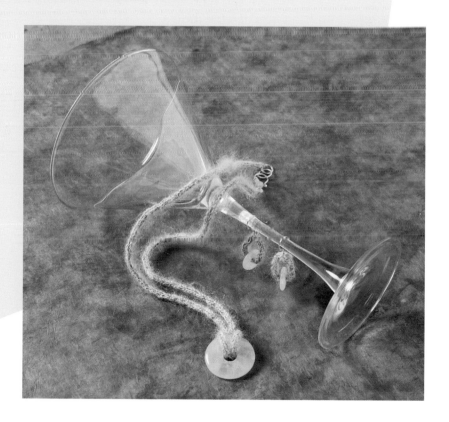

Acknowledgments

This book would not be possible without the many people who have supported us. Thank you all!

Thanks to Mary Ann Hall for guiding us through the process of publishing our first books. Thank you Rochelle Bourgault and Regina Grenier for keeping things running smoothly and designing a book layout that we're proud of. The Rockport team worked their magic with this book and hopefully had as much fun as we did. A big thanks to Sue McCain for your excellent technical editing, and to Judy Love for bringing the techniques to life with your illustrations. It's been a pleasure working with you.

Thanks a million to our families. Our husbands helped tremendously in many ways. Our parents did, too.

We are very thankful for everyone's patience and understanding while we concentrated on writing this book. Thanks to our children whose laughter and kisses brighten every day. We love you!

Thank you to Elena at Garden District Needlework Shop in New Orleans. You got the yarn ball rolling!

We appreciate all of the companies listed in the resource section who provided superb products for the designs—luscious yarns, sparkling beads, and fabulous people.

Thank you, Claire Wudowsky, for your friendship and your big, giant brain.

And a toast to you, knitters. Keep creating extraordinary beauty through ordinary means.